Food &

OTHER THINGS I LOVE

Food &
OTHER THINGS I LOVE

MORE THAN
100
ITALIAN
AMERICAN
RECIPES
FROM MY
FAMILY TO
YOURS

CAROLINE MANZO

WITH **CASEY ELSASS**

Photography by Lauren Volo

CHRONICLE BOOKS
SAN FRANCISCO

◆◆◆◆◆◆◆◆◆◆

Library of Congress Cataloging-in-Publication Data available.

ISBN 978-1-7972-2525-8

Manufactured in China.

Design by Laura Palese.

Typesetting by Laura Palese. Typeset in Basetica, Caslon Doric, Caslon Italian, ED Frogmore, Grotta, and Sign Maker JNL.

Cento is a registered trademark of Alanric Food Distributors, Inc. College Inn is a registered trademark of Del Monte Foods, Inc. Diamond Crystal is a registered trademark of Cargill Inc. Frangelico is a registered trademark of Davide Campari-Milano N.V. Mutti is a registered trademark of MUTTI S.p.A. Nutella is a registered trademark of FERRERO S.P.A. Oreo is a registered trademark of Intercontinental Great Brands. Progresso is a registered trademark of Pet Incorporated. Rao's is a registered trademark of Rao's Restaurant Group, LLC. Taylor Ham is a registered trademark of Taylor Provisions Company. Tito's Handmade Vodka is a registered trademark of Fifth Generation Inc.

10 9 8 7 6 5 4 3 2 1

Chronicle books and gifts are available at special quantity discounts to corporations, professional associations, literacy programs, and other organizations. For details and discount information, please contact our premiums department at corporatesales@chroniclebooks.com or at 1-800-759-0190.

Chronicle Books LLC
680 Second Street
San Francisco, California 94107
www.chroniclebooks.com

To my husband, Albert; my children, Albie, Lauren, Christopher, and Chelsea; and my granddaughter, Markie. You are my world and the loves of my life. If I can leave you with anything as my legacy, it would be to continue with tradition and fill your homes with love, laughter, good health, good food, and family. If you have that, you've got everything.

ALL MY LOVE NOW AND ALWAYS,
CAROLINE / MOM / DEEDEE
XOXO

Contents

STAPLES

Lazy MORNINGS

Warm & COZY

Something SWEET

Late Night SNACKS

Intro

◆◆◆◆◆◆◆◆◆

At some point in life, you find your first love, and your heart is forever changed. I found two first loves, and they happened at the same time. They were, in no particular order, food and family. When you're Italian American, it's almost impossible to separate the two.

Family time and mealtime have always been one and the same for me. When we eat, we gather, we talk, we argue, we laugh, and we share the same stories we've been telling for years. When we cook, we pass knowledge from one generation to the next, we swat hands away, and we shoo husbands out of the kitchen. Food is more than just food; it's our history, our story, our memories, and our heritage.

I was born and raised in Queens, one of eleven kids. In the summers, my family would escape the city heat to our farm upstate. We had a vegetable garden bursting with produce, and my parents, grandparents, aunts, and uncles seemed to live in the kitchen. It was in that farmhouse that I had my earliest cooking lessons, when my nose could barely reach the counter. My family taught me to use a little of this, a little of that, and whatever we had around to make magic in the kitchen. But it was our time together as a family that taught me the connection between food and love. We didn't always have a lot, but we had each other, we had the food on our table, and that was more than enough.

I share those same traditions with my family now, and my house in New Jersey is home base. Every Sunday, I have an army of hungry family and friends barging through the door. Every baby in my family has had a broken-up meatball as their first introduction to solid food, with a crowd of aunts, uncles, and cousins cheering them on. On Christmas Eve, my house fills with family and friends (fifty people on a slow year). Morning, noon, and night, all year round, family and friends are dropping by to eat, gossip, and unwind.

> 66 Food is more than just food; it's our history, our story, our memories, and our heritage.

66 My cooking is simple, no bells and whistles.

When I'm at the table, eating my favorite things, surrounded by my favorite people, it's like a hug for my soul.

My cooking is simple, no bells and whistles. I cook from intuition, from the secrets my family taught me, and from the experience of a lifetime in the kitchen. And while it may not always look magazine ready, I'll tell you what: My food is extremely delicious. This book is packed to the brim with family recipes perfected over time, culinary wisdom passed through generations, and memories made around the table. It's also packed with tips and tricks, with plenty of room to scribble notes, and you have my full permission to adjust to your tastes. I want you to get comfortable with these recipes, put them in your rotation, and cook them until they start to feel like your own.

But first things first: I believe every kitchen has to be in working order so cooking can feel easy and fun! The Kitchen Arsenal (see page 20) will give you everything you need to arm yourself for battle against a hungry army. The Value of a Good Pantry (see page 27) is what I've learned to always keep in stock so meals can appear out of thin air. And throughout the book, I'll share my advice on how to Set a Beautiful Table (see page 48) and Cook for a Crowd (see page 72), plus why you should Make Your Apron Fabulous (see page 100), Decorate Your House (see page 130), and Celebrate Every Moment (see page 170).

When it comes to cooking, we'll get started with Staples, the little things like Pesto Two Ways (page 33), Roasted Red Peppers (page 39), and Garlic Bread (page 41) that are always at the ready to act as my building blocks for improvising a meal. When it comes to the first meal of the day, I like to take it easy, which is where Lazy Mornings comes in. Classics like Potatoes & Eggs on a Roll (page 47) and Taylor Ham & Cheese (page 60) are alongside some of my best hacks for making breakfast easy, like Baking Dish Frittata (page 51) and Slow Cooker Oatmeal (page 52).

Warm & Cozy is for filling your house with inviting smells and filling your table with delicious meals. This chapter includes recipes like Escarole & Bean Soup (page 64), Penne with Vodka Sauce (page 69), Creamy Broccoli Cavatelli (page 70), Deep-Dish Sausage Pizza Pie (page 84), and, my favorite when no one can make up their mind, Whole F**king Chicken (page 80). Al Fresco takes the party outdoors for my favorite meals on the grill, like Smoky Grilled Peaches (page 95), Grilled Chicken Wings with Balsamic Barbecue Sauce (page 106), and Italian Hot Dogs (page 113), plus some of my favorites when we're down the shore, like Smothered Corn Cobs (page 88), Sour Cream Potato Salad (page 99), and Linguine with Clams (page 119).

Molto Buono is a celebration of classic Italian cooking with the things you'd expect—Ultimate Chicken Parm (page 132), Slow-Braised Braciole (page 136), Sunday Gravy (page 144)—and a few of my personal classics—Burrata with Prosciutto & Red Peppers (page 123), Chicken under a Brick (page 135), and Manzo Meatballs (page 139). If you know me, you know my house comes alive during the holidays and my kitchen goes into overdrive. Home for the Holidays arms you with everything you need to feed a crowd, like a guide to building the dream Antipasti Spread (page 153), a perfect Thanksgiving Stuffing (page 165), Extreme Mashed Potatoes (page 167), and my favorite late-night Christmas Eve tradition, Mussels Marinara with Garlic Bread (page 174).

I believe in life you're either a baker or a cook—you can truly master only one. (I'll give you one guess which one I am.) Something Sweet is my celebration of taking the easy way out with dessert. Things like Pumpkin Banana "Pudding" (page 178), Slow Cooker Rice Pudding (page 179), and Spiked Fruit Salad with Mascarpone Dip (page 199) are so easy I could do them in my sleep. When I'm feeling generous and ready to turn the oven on, I have Deep, Dark Chocolate Pudding Cake (page 180), Almond Macaroon Cookies (page 185), and my absolute favorite dessert, Aunt Red's Cheesecake (page 183), passed down from my dad's favorite aunt. Finally, because we never stop eating in my house, I have all my favorite Late Night Snacks. The comfort of Spaghetti Aglio e Olio (page 202) and English Muffin Pizza (page 209) and the fun of Nutella Pizza (page 212) and Adult Root Beer Float (page 217) will send everyone off to bed full and happy.

Food & Other Things I Love is more than just a collection of recipes; it's a celebration of my family and who we are. It's my memories of my grandparents, my parents, my husband, and my kids. It's a testament to eating well, loving hard, and laughing along the way. Every dish in this book has a story to tell, carries a little piece of my history, and reminds me of the people I love the most. I can't wait for you to share this food with your own family and friends, as you build your own memories, meals, and magic with the people you love the most.

THE KITCHEN ARSENAL

Preparation is the foundation of everything! Whether it's a coffee-fueled breakfast on the go or Sunday with family in the kitchen, having your arsenal of tools (and knowing how to use them) makes all the difference. Having your meat thermometer at the ready before the meat hits the heat, arming yourself with a good cast-iron skillet (and knowing how to take care of it), and always keeping extra Tupperware around are just a few of the things I've learned after decades on the front lines.

DON'T BREAK THE BANK

These are the cheap and easy items that every kitchen should have.

CAN OPENER: I use a lot of canned tomatoes and beans, so I always have my sturdy opener nearby.

CUTTING BOARD: I like having a couple of big, sturdy cutting boards around. That way you can hand one off as you're delegating to the troops. Pro tip: Wet a paper towel and squeeze it dry. Lay the towel flat, then set your board on top. Instant nonslip grip!

GRATERS: I keep a box grater for larger shreds of cheese and a rasp-style grater for finely grating cheese and garlic or zesting citrus.

LADLE: You immediately think of soups, but a ladle is also great when you need to split things evenly, like pouring pancakes, spreading sauces, and dividing batter.

LOTS AND LOTS OF FOOD STORAGE: I always have airtight containers, zip-top bags, and washed-out delivery containers ready to go. They're perfect for sending guests home with leftovers, packing lunches, and freezing extra batches.

MEASURING CUPS: Look for a set of dry measuring cups that go from ¼ cup [60 g] to 1 cup [240 g]. (Fun fact: If you have an ⅛ cup measure, that's the same as 2 Tbsp.) You'll also need a liquid measuring cup. I have separate 1 cup [240 ml], 2 cup [480 ml], and 4 cup [960 ml] measures, but decide what you need based on kitchen space.

MEASURING SPOONS: Look for a set that goes from ¼ tsp to 1 Tbsp.

MIXING BOWLS: I can never have enough mixing bowls around. Stainless steel is my favorite for easy cleaning and durability, and you can easily find a set of all different sizes that neatly stack.

OVEN MITTS AND HOT PAD: A good set of oven mitts is a cook's best friend. And a few hot pads to scatter around the counter are equally important.

PLASTIC WRAP, ALUMINUM FOIL, AND PARCHMENT PAPER: If you're in the kitchen often, buy in bulk!

ROLLING PIN: A handy tool for chasing anyone out of the kitchen. Plus it can roll dough, crush crackers, tenderize meat, smash spices, crush ice, and grind spices. Endless possibilities!

SILICONE SPATULA: Not the pancake flipper, but the smaller, sleeker spatula. It's perfect for sautéing, mixing, folding, and scraping.

SPIDER SKIMMER: This skimmer is like a slotted spoon on steroids. (Although a big slotted spoon will work just fine in a pinch.) It's my favorite tool for frying foods.

THERMOMETERS: I like to have two: a digital instant-read thermometer for checking meat temperatures and a clip-on candy thermometer for deep-frying or making sweets. It's worth having both to send the right one in for the job.

TONGS: I like the ones with silicone tips to protect my nonstick cookware, but I keep a metal pair for the grill. Just make sure they're long enough that you don't singe any arm hair in the process.

VEGETABLE PEELER: I use mine for a lot more than just vegetables. I like to grate big pieces of Parmesan for pasta, shave chocolate onto a dessert, or peel lemon rinds for cocktails.

WHISK: A big classic whisk will get the job done every time.

WOODEN SPOON: Gentle enough to stir, strong enough to swat away invaders. It wouldn't be an Italian kitchen without a wooden spoon.

INVESTMENT PROPERTIES

Spending a little extra on quality items will ensure
a long and happy life with your tools.

BAKING PANS: A 9 by 13 in [23 by 33 cm] rectangular pan, an 8 by 8 in [20 by 20 cm] square pan, a 5 by 9 in [13 by 23 cm] loaf pan, and an 8 in [20 cm] cake pan are the dream team for baking projects. They'll get you through everything sweet and savory, no problem!

BLENDER AND FOOD PROCESSOR: A blender will whip up homemade dressing, sauces, and dips in no time. A food processor will save time on chopping, mixing, and even making dough.

COOKIE SCOOPS: These usually come in a set of small (about 2 tsp), medium (about 1½ Tbsp), and large (about 3 Tbsp). They're perfect for portioning cookies, dividing muffin batter, making pancakes, scooping ice cream, and even rolling the perfect meatball.

DUTCH OVEN: My go-to heavy-duty pot for slow-cooking sauces, braising meats, and making soups. It can slide from the stove right into the oven.

HANDHELD MIXER: Give your arm a break and grab one of these for creaming butter, whipping cream, or beating egg whites.

KNIVES: A strong, 8 in [20 cm] chef's knife has pretty much become part of my hand. Make sure it feels comfortable and secure in your grip—you'll be using it a lot. A large serrated knife is a perfect partner, ideal for sawing through crusty bread or slicing ripe tomatoes. Finally, a paring knife is great for smaller, precise tasks like trimming. Just remember, a dull knife is a dangerous knife because it's more likely to slip against the food and cut you. Invest in a good knife sharpener to keep them in shape or have them professionally sharpened regularly.

LARGE CAST-IRON SKILLET: I pull this baby out when I need a hard sear on meats or want to move back and forth between the stove and oven (or even the grill). Investing in a good 12 in [30.5 cm] skillet (and taking care of it) is an investment for yourself and even future generations. To clean your cast-iron skillet, let it cool slightly, then use warm water and a skillet brush to get the surface clean. For any stuck-on bits, use a mixture of kosher salt and a splash of vegetable oil to scrub. Dish soap can be your last resort. It will strip off some of the seasoning but won't hurt the skillet. After it's clean, set over high heat to dry completely. Swirl in some vegetable oil and let it smoke. Remove from the heat and use a wad of paper towels to wipe out the excess oil. Cool completely before storing.

LARGE, MEDIUM, AND SMALL SAUCEPANS: Great for making sauces, boiling pasta, reheating leftovers, and so much more.

LARGE NONSTICK SKILLET: My teammate for sautéing vegetables, frying eggs, and searing meats with no sticky situations. These don't last as long as other cookware, so look for a good one that's not too expensive.

PASTA MAKER: When it's time to get serious, a pasta maker is the essential tool in the Italian kitchen. Enjoy freshly rolled and cut pasta any time you want!

PASTA POT WITH A STRAINER INSERT: Let's keep it practical. A big pasta pot that comes with its own strainer will make it easy to go from pot to skillet while saving all that good, starchy pasta water. Plus the strainer can be used just like you'd use a colander, perfect for draining or washing any ingredients.

RIMMED BAKING SHEET: A half sheet pan is about 18 by 13 in [46 by 33 cm], which will easily fit in your oven but still give you plenty of room for ingredients. Find a thick, sturdy baking sheet for perfect browning.

THE VALUE OF
A GOOD PANTRY

Similar to keeping a well-equipped kitchen, having a pantry that is ready to tackle anything will help you breeze through everything from a quick weeknight dinner to welcoming fifty people over on Christmas Eve. Here are the top ten things I'm never without:

CANNED BEANS: I always have a stack of cannellini beans in my pantry. These starchy proteins are perfect for boosting soups, pastas, and vegetables. Progresso is my go-to brand, but I'll always grab whatever is on sale that week.

CANNED TOMATOES: Tomatoes are the backbone of Italian American cooking. Stock up on whole peeled tomatoes, crushed tomatoes, and tomato sauce for flavorful sauces, soups, and stews. My favorite brands are Cento and Mutti.

CHEESE: I always have big hunks of Parmesan and pecorino around for finishing pastas, risottos, salads, and soups. Plus the rind is a flavor bomb you can add anytime you're simmering sauce or broth on the stove. Any good Parmigiano-Reggiano will work, but for my pecorino, I stick to the Locatelli brand for an extra savory punch.

CHICKEN STOCK: I always go for stock, which is made from bones and has a richer flavor and slightly thicker texture. (I also almost always add a splash of white wine for some acidity to round it out.) My favorite is the cans of College Inn, but plenty of brands of boxed stock are just as good.

DRIED PASTA: No pantry is complete without a variety of pasta shapes, such as spaghetti, linguine, angel hair, lasagna, penne, orecchiette, and macaroni. I like to splurge on the more expensive pastas from Eataly when company is coming, but for a normal night I love grocery brands like De Cecco and Barilla.

OILS AND FATS: A great extra-virgin olive oil is a must for adding depth and richness to sauces, dressings, and marinades and roasting meats and vegetables. I keep one lighter-flavored olive oil for cooking and one more assertive olive oil for finishing. I also keep a neutral oil, like vegetable oil, around for super high intensity cooking and frying. And finally, unsalted butter is my star player when I want a little more creaminess in the mix.

ONION AND GARLIC: Whenever someone pops in the kitchen and asks what smells so good, it's almost always because onion and garlic have just hit the oil. It's a smell like no other and always my starting point for savory cooking.

SEASONINGS: These include plenty of kosher salt (I prefer Diamond Crystal), black peppercorns for freshly grinding (it really makes a difference!), red pepper flakes when I want a little heat, and dried oregano for an herby hit. I also keep fresh herbs like basil, rosemary, and thyme on hand at all times, either in my garden or stored in my fridge.

VINEGARS AND LEMONS: Perfect for drizzling over salads or roasted veggies, mixing into marinades, or reducing for glazes. Balsamic vinegar and red wine vinegar are my two staples to keep nearby, and I always have a few lemons around for a lighter touch of acidity to finish off fish and pasta.

WINE: A good bottle of wine is great company in the kitchen, not only for sipping but also for adding tons of flavor. A dry white and a full-bodied red—something drinkable but not overly expensive—are perfect.

BONUS ROUND: In my freezer, I'll always have some leftover sauces, a few batches of soup, a lasagna or two, and some homemade pasta. But most importantly, I always keep bags of frozen vegetables and Italian sausages. The vegetables are fresh no matter what season we're in and can be added to anything hot to quickly thaw and immediately bulk up the dish. I thaw the sausages in a pot of hot water and then have an instant flavor-packed protein to add to a soup or pasta.

Staples

••••••••••

These are all of my favorite

homemade seasonings, sauces, condiments, and garnishes. Most of them can be made at least a week in advance, which means my fridge is always stocked. In my house, Sunday is the day when the gravy (or red sauce for those who would never call it gravy!) is simmering, the garlic is roasting, and the peppers are marinating, but any day of the week is a perfect time to build your staples!

POTATO SALAD *Seasoning*

MAKES / ½ CUP [100 G]

My son Christopher and I are mad scientists in the kitchen. We're always digging around and inventing things together. Some of our favorite things to make are batches of rubs to have on hand, which are especially useful when we're cooking for crowds. We invented this potato salad seasoning years ago, and it's an easy way to punch up anything. This goes in my Sour Cream Potato Salad (page 99) but can also be used to season chicken, fish, or veggies.

¼ cup [45 g] yellow mustard seeds (see Note)

4 tsp freshly ground black pepper

1 Tbsp celery salt

1 Tbsp garlic salt

2 tsp onion powder

In a medium bowl, whisk the mustard seeds, black pepper, celery salt, garlic salt, and onion powder together. Transfer to an airtight container and store in a cool, dry place for up to 3 months.

NOTE

If you have a spice grinder, give the mustard seeds one or two pulses to open up the flavor.

PESTO
Two Ways

MAKES / **1 CUP [240 ML]**

For years, I've been keeping an herb garden at my house. And anyone who grows herbs will tell you that nothing grows more abundantly than basil and mint. So of course, my fridge and freezer are always stocked with plenty of pesto. It's a versatile and useful thing to have on hand, perfect for punching up any pasta, grilled meats, roasted veggies, or even salad dressings. Here are my recipes for a classic pesto using basil and a fresh, aromatic mint pesto that's maybe even better!

CLASSIC PESTO

2 cups [24 g] packed fresh basil leaves

½ cup [60 g] toasted pine nuts

6 garlic cloves

½ cup [30 g] grated pecorino
or ½ cup [15 g] Parmesan cheese

1 tsp kosher salt

½ tsp freshly ground black pepper

6 Tbsp [90 ml] extra-virgin olive oil

In a food processor, combine the basil, pine nuts, and garlic. Pulse about six times, stopping to scrape down the sides as needed, until the ingredients are finely chopped. Add the pecorino, salt, and pepper and pulse about two more times until combined. With the processor running, slowly pour in the olive oil in a steady stream. Taste for seasoning before using or transferring to an airtight container.

MINT PESTO

1 cup [12 g] packed fresh mint leaves

1 cup [12 g] packed fresh basil leaves

½ cup [6 g] packed fresh parsley leaves

4 green onions, white and green parts

2 garlic cloves

Zest of 1 lemon

1 tsp kosher salt

½ tsp freshly ground black pepper

¼ cup [60 ml] extra-virgin olive oil

In a food processor, combine the mint, basil, parsley, green onions, and garlic. Pulse about six times, stopping to scrape down the sides as needed, until the ingredients are finely chopped. Add the lemon zest, salt, and pepper and pulse about two more times until combined. With the processor running, slowly pour in the olive oil in a steady stream. Taste for seasoning before using or transferring to an airtight container.

NOTE: Both pestos will keep in the refrigerator for up to 5 days. But I like to make big batches and freeze them instead. Pesto can be frozen in glass jars or an airtight container—just be sure to leave some room for expansion as it freezes. It will keep for up to 6 months and can be thawed overnight in the refrigerator before using.

LEMON *Aioli*

MAKES / ¾ CUP [180 G]

This easy take on an aioli uses pantry ingredients to create something that tastes like it took much more effort. I serve it alongside my Grilled Artichokes (page 92) in the summer, but it's perfect all year round alongside lamb or any rich meats, with roasted vegetables, or just for dipping french fries.

⅓ cup [80 g] mayonnaise

⅓ cup [80 g] low-fat Greek yogurt

4 tsp fresh lemon juice

2 garlic cloves, minced

¼ tsp kosher salt

2 tsp sliced basil or mint (optional)

In a small bowl, whisk together the mayonnaise, yogurt, lemon juice, garlic, and salt. Cover with plastic wrap and refrigerate until ready to use, or refrigerate in an airtight container for up to 5 days. Fold in the herbs (if using) just before serving.

GARLIC *Confit*

My husband, Al, came home one day with the idea in his head that he was craving garlic confit. I had never made it, so we looked it up, tried it, and loved it, and the rest is history. I always have jars and jars of the stuff lying around, perfect for smashing the soft cloves into a salad dressing, using the oil to roast vegetables, scattering the whole cloves over chicken—really anywhere you'd be using garlic anyway.

3 cups [500 g] garlic cloves
3 cups [710 ml] extra-virgin
   olive oil

Preheat the oven to 350°F [180°C].

In a 9 by 13 in [23 by 33 cm] baking pan, spread the garlic cloves in an even layer, then pour in the olive oil until the cloves are completely submerged. Bake for 40 to 45 minutes, until the garlic is golden brown. Set on a rack to cool completely in the pan, then transfer the garlic and oil to an airtight container. Refrigerate for up to 2 weeks.

Tapenade

MAKES / ½ CUP [120 G]

It's always a good idea to keep tapenade around at all times. When someone unexpectedly pops in, it's a perfect thing to serve with crackers. A thick spread of it over chicken or fish is divine. Mix it with Lemon Aioli (page 34) and spread it on a sandwich. It's even perfect simply tossed with pasta.

1 cup [140 g] pitted olives of choice, such as Kalamata, Castelvetrano, or a mix

4 garlic cloves

2 Tbsp drained capers

Zest and juice of 1 lemon

3 Tbsp extra-virgin olive oil

In a food processor, combine the olives, garlic, and capers. Pulse six to eight times, stopping to scrape down the sides as needed, until they're finely chopped. Transfer to a medium bowl and stir in the lemon zest and juice and the olive oil. Serve immediately or refrigerate in an airtight container for up to 1 week.

Long Hots

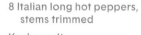

SERVES / 4

Italian long hots are a *must* in my house. They're like shishito peppers: Most of them are mild, but once in a while you get a live one! We eat them as an antipasto with some bread for dipping, or warmed up as a side for pork or chicken, and Al usually eats them straight out of the fridge as a midday snack. One time he finished the last pepper and watched me cover the container and put it back in the fridge. "What are you doing?!" he asked, thinking I had finally lost it. "That's good oil!" I said, excited to cook with all the flavorful juices still at the bottom.

½ cup [120 ml] extra-virgin olive oil

6 garlic cloves, crushed or minced

8 Italian long hot peppers, stems trimmed

Kosher salt

In a large skillet over medium heat, heat the olive oil. When the oil shimmers, add the garlic. Sauté, stirring occasionally, until the garlic is golden brown, about 4 minutes. Add the peppers and a good pinch of salt. Stir to coat the peppers in oil. Cover the skillet, turn the heat to low, and simmer for about 20 minutes, stirring occasionally and flipping halfway, until the peppers are very soft. Serve immediately or refrigerate in an airtight container for up to 1 week.

Baked TOMATOES

MAKES / **8 TOMATO HALVES**

4 large, firm vine tomatoes (see Note)

Kosher salt and freshly ground black pepper

½ cup [70 g] seasoned bread crumbs

2 Tbsp finely chopped fresh parsley

2 garlic cloves, minced

Extra-virgin olive oil, for drizzling

This is simple cooking, no bells and whistles, but extremely delicious. I keep the tomatoes in the fridge so I can spread them on a sandwich, pile them on fish, warm them up with eggs, mash them into a meatloaf, or just reheat them as an emergency side dish.

Preheat the oven to 400°F [200°C]. Lightly oil a 9 by 13 in [23 by 33 cm] baking pan.

Cut the tomatoes in half and arrange the halves, cut-side up, in the prepared baking pan. Season with a good pinch of salt and pepper.

In a small bowl, stir together the bread crumbs, parsley, and garlic. Divide the mixture evenly over the tomatoes, about 1 Tbsp per tomato, then drizzle lightly with olive oil.

Bake for 15 to 20 minutes, until the tomatoes are tender and the topping is golden brown. Serve immediately or refrigerate in an airtight container for up to 1 week.

Buy tomatoes in a similar size so they all cook evenly. To keep the halves steady as they bake, I trim a little off the rounded side of each half to make a flat surface.

Roasted RED PEPPERS

6 red bell peppers

½ cup [120 ml] extra-virgin olive oil

4 garlic cloves, thinly sliced

Kosher salt and freshly ground black pepper

MAKES / **2 CUPS [440 G]**

◆◆◆◆◆◆◆◆◆◆◆◆◆◆◆◆◆◆◆◆◆◆◆◆◆◆◆◆◆◆

I'll admit it: I'll grab a jar of roasted red peppers in a pinch or when they're on sale. But it's a sin because homemade freshly roasted peppers are just *so much better*. Plus, who doesn't love playing with fire? I like to toss the peppers in a salad, spread them on a pizza, mix them with eggs, stir them into a soup, or pulse them in a blender for an automatic pasta sauce. But for me, the best part is opening the bag of steamed peppers. Nothing smells as good as a batch of homemade peppers.

◆◆◆◆◆◆◆◆◆◆◆◆◆◆◆◆◆◆◆◆◆◆◆◆◆◆◆◆◆◆

Set a gas burner to high heat. (This can also be done on the grill.) Use tongs to place one of the peppers directly on the flame. Flip the pepper until all sides are blistered and black, about 1 minute. Transfer to a brown paper bag or zip-top bag. Close tightly and repeat with the remaining peppers. Let all the peppers steam in the bag until they're easy to handle, about 30 minutes.

Peel each pepper. Discard the stems, seeds, and blackened skins. Thinly slice the peppers. In a 1 pt [450 g] jar, combine the peppers, olive oil, garlic, and a generous pinch of salt and pepper. Cover the jar tightly and lightly shake to combine. Refrigerate for up to 1 week.

Garlic BREAD

SERVES / 6 TO 8

½ cup [113 g] unsalted butter, at room temperature

6 garlic cloves

½ cup [15 g] grated Parmesan cheese

¼ tsp kosher salt

¼ tsp freshly ground black pepper

1 large loaf Italian bread

2 Tbsp finely chopped fresh parsley

◆◆◆◆◆◆◆◆◆◆◆◆◆◆◆◆◆◆◆◆◆◆◆◆◆

When I'm serving dinner, there is always bread on the table. Sometimes the meal is perfect with just a good plain crusty loaf. But most of the time, the table isn't complete without a loaf of garlic bread. I make mine big with a simple garlic butter mixture on top, the classic style. Years ago, Christopher decided to throw some cheese on top, just a few scraps we had lying around in the fridge, and the tradition stuck. My family calls it Sexy Bread because that gorgeous cheese pull makes the bread so much better. Whenever I'm making this recipe, I always ask, "Should I make it classic or make it sexy?"

◆◆◆◆◆◆◆◆◆◆◆◆◆◆◆◆◆◆◆◆◆◆◆◆◆

Preheat the oven to 400°F [200°C]. Line a rimmed baking sheet with parchment paper.

In a food processor, combine the butter, garlic, Parmesan, salt, and pepper. Process until the garlic is chopped and everything is combined, about 1 minute. Scrape down the sides and pulse two more times to combine.

Cut the Italian bread in half horizontally like a sandwich, but don't cut all the way through. Fan open the bread and lay it flat on the prepared baking sheet. Use a rubber spatula to spread the butter mixture evenly over the entire surface of the bread. Transfer to the oven and bake for about 10 minutes, until the bread is crispy and golden. Cut into large pieces and garnish with the parsley before serving.

MAKE IT Sexy Bread

Once the butter mixture is spread over the bread, layer on 2 cups [240 g] of crumbled blue cheese, 8 oz [230 g] of sliced provolone, 2 cups [160 g] of shredded sharp Cheddar, 1 lb [455 g] of sliced low-moisture mozzarella, or some combo of all of those. Bake for 10 to 15 minutes, until the cheese is nicely melted.

Lazy Mornings

I like to start the day right, whether I'm cooking for a crowd or need something easy just for myself. But no matter what, it has to be unbelievably easy because mornings are meant to be lazy!

Truffle
ASPARAGUS
WITH FRIED EGG

SERVES / 4

1½ lb [680 g] asparagus

2 Tbsp extra-virgin olive oil

Kosher salt and freshly ground black pepper

2 Tbsp unsalted butter

4 eggs

Truffle oil and Parmesan cheese, for serving

I'm not a fancy person, but we all deserve a little luxury once in a while. And when I say luxury, I'm talking a tiny drizzle of truffle oil, which makes anything feel like an event without breaking the bank. Giuseppe Ristorante Italiano, one of my favorite spots in New Jersey, inspired this easy breakfast of roasted asparagus and fried eggs, which is more than the sum of its parts, with lots of great flavors and textures mingling together. I like to roast my asparagus until it's just barely tender and still has snap to it, and I like my egg yolk soft and oozy. It's up to you how much grated Parmesan to add on top, but for a breakfast this good, I say live a little!

Preheat the oven to 425°F [220°C]. Line a rimmed baking sheet with aluminum foil.

Trim the woody ends off the asparagus, about 1 in [2.5 cm] from the base. If the spears are thick, use a vegetable peeler to remove the tough peel from the bottom half. Arrange the spears in an even layer on the prepared baking sheet and toss with the olive oil and a big pinch of salt and pepper. Transfer to the oven and roast for 10 to 12 minutes, until the asparagus is crisp-tender.

About 5 minutes before the asparagus is done, heat two medium skillets over medium heat. Melt 1 Tbsp of butter in each skillet, then crack 2 eggs in each, giving them plenty of space to fry. Cover the pans and cook for 2 minutes, then uncover and fry for 2 to 3 minutes more until the whites are opaque but the yolks are still runny.

Divide the asparagus among four plates and top each with a fried egg. Season the eggs with a little salt and pepper and a small drizzle of truffle oil. Grate a little or a lot of Parmesan over the dish and serve immediately.

EGG *in the* HOLE

SERVES / 1

1 slice sandwich bread

1 Tbsp unsalted butter

1 egg

Kosher salt and freshly
ground black pepper

My grandma and mom used to make this for me when I was sick. It's very simple, just a slice of bread and an egg, but it felt like an extra big hug. I was one of eleven kids, so it took more time to make than the skillet of scrambled eggs everyone else had to fight over—it was the attention and care through cooking that felt so great. I make it for my family more often now, but it's still my go-to when someone I love is feeling down.

Use a small drinking glass or cookie cutter to cut a hole from the center of the bread. (Save the round!) In a small nonstick skillet over medium heat, melt the butter. Lay the slice of bread in the skillet and set the round next to it. Crack the egg into the hole and season with a good pinch of salt and pepper. Fry until the bread is golden brown on the bottom, about 2 minutes. Flip the bread (and the round). Fry for another 2 minutes for a runny yolk or about 4 minutes for a firm yolk. Transfer everything to a plate and use the toasted round for dipping!

POTATOES & EGGS ON A Roll

SERVES / 4

2 Tbsp plus 2 tsp extra-virgin olive oil

1 medium russet potato, peeled and cut into 1/2 in [13 mm] cubes

1 medium white onion, thinly sliced

Kosher salt

6 eggs

4 kaiser semolina rolls, split and toasted

Potatoes and eggs are a hard-core Italian family staple. My dad's mom would haul in dozens of eggs and a big bag of potatoes and make a huge batch of this for my siblings, cousins, aunts, and uncles. I can still hear everyone shouting and fighting over a roll packed with warm, comforting potatoes and eggs, followed by silence while we all ate in bliss. I keep the tradition alive to this day, making a big batch of it on Sunday mornings and watching it get cleared out within minutes. This recipe calls for serving the potato and egg on rolls, but I also like mine on white sandwich bread, not even toasted, so it gets gooey and gummy as I eat it. It also doesn't have to be just a breakfast dish; it's just as good in the middle of the afternoon or as a hearty midnight snack.

In a large nonstick skillet over medium-high heat, heat 2 Tbsp of the olive oil. When the oil shimmers, add the potato and cook, tossing, until lightly browned and beginning to soften, 4 to 5 minutes. Add the onion and season with a good pinch of salt. Cook, stirring occasionally, until the potato is cooked through and the onion is browned but not completely soft, 8 to 10 minutes.

Meanwhile, in a medium bowl, beat the eggs with a big pinch of salt. Turn the heat to low and give the pan a moment to cool. Pour in the eggs and cook, stirring constantly, until just set, 2 to 3 minutes. Remove from the heat and taste for seasoning. Divide among the rolls and serve piping hot.

SET A Beautiful TABLE

My food is not pretty, and I'm not embarrassed to admit it! I put all my love and attention into food that tastes great, but precise plating is not in my DNA. I just don't have the patience for it. The one place I don't compromise, however, is a beautifully set table.

A beautifully set table is like a perfectly wrapped present: It tells you this is something special. It doesn't have to be ornate or over-the-top or expensive, and I actually prefer using mismatched dishware, silverware, and décor for a little character. When the table is set just the right way, it draws everyone in and makes them feel welcome. Here are my five rules for a perfect table setting:

1 **A POP OF COLOR IS BETTER THAN TECHNICOLOR.** I like to keep things pretty neutral with a few splashes of color, even if it's just vibrant flowers and pillar candles in the center, or setting out napkins with a personality.

2 **MIX AND MATCH.** I like to layer different textures and styles and even mismatched plates and silverware to keep it interesting and individual. In my mind, a silk napkin, a macramé place mat, and a colorful pressed glass goblet all make sense together. I like to mix high and low too—I'll plop a $4 vase on the table next to my freshly polished good silver.

3 **EVERYTHING IN ITS PLACE.** Getting organized helps give the table a sense of purpose. Some meals just need a fork and a knife, but when I'm doing a full setting, I remember this guide. Dinner plates go in the center of each place setting, with salad plates and bread plates to the left. Silverware goes in the order it will be used, from the outside in, with forks to the left, knives on the right (blade facing inward), and soup spoons to the right of the knives. Water glasses go above the knives with wineglasses next to them.

4 **FAMILY FIRST.** I skip store-bought items in favor of things handed down through my family, because they actually mean something. Our heirlooms are nothing fancy, but they hold a lot of sentimental value and remind us of everyone who is with us at the table in spirit. My daughter and my niece are currently fighting over my meatball bowl. It's a basic stainless-steel bowl with a dent on the side, but it's been my designated meatball bowl their whole lives, and I know one day it'll continue to live on at their shared tables.

5 **THE FINISHING TOUCHES.** Move any clutter or distractions away from the table, so the focus stays on each other and the meal you're about to enjoy. I also run through everything in my head so I can make sure all the condiments, glasses, and serving utensils are ready and waiting on the table. It saves me from getting up and down a hundred times and keeps us all present in the moment.

BAKING DISH *Frittata*

SERVES / 8

---

2 medium russet potatoes, thinly sliced

1 medium bell pepper, thinly sliced

1 small zucchini, cubed

4 Tbsp [60 ml] olive oil

Kosher salt and freshly ground black pepper

1 large green onion, white and green parts, chopped

1 small shallot, thinly sliced

2 garlic cloves, thinly sliced

1 medium tomato, thinly sliced

10 eggs

1/2 cup [15 g] grated Parmesan cheese

1/3 cup [80 ml] whole milk

1 Tbsp finely chopped fresh parsley

1 sprig fresh rosemary leaves

1 sprig fresh thyme leaves

When it's summer and I don't feel like cooking a massive breakfast every day, I turn to this easy dish. It's a frittata on a big scale, so I usually make two batches at the same time, cut it up, and throw it in the fridge to serve throughout the week. (Like most things, it tastes better every day it sits and the flavors meld together.) It's a rare breakfast that's equally good reheated on the go or steaming hot out of the oven to sit down and eat together.

Preheat the oven to 350°F [180°C]. Grease the bottom and sides of a 9 by 13 in [23 by 33 cm] baking pan.

In the baking pan, toss the potatoes, pepper, zucchini, and olive oil until completely coated. Season with a pinch of salt and pepper. Bake in the oven until the potatoes can be easily pierced with a fork, about 15 minutes. Remove from the oven and stir in the green onion, shallot, and garlic. Layer the tomato slices over the vegetables.

In a large bowl, lightly beat the eggs. Whisk in the Parmesan, milk, parsley, and a big pinch of salt and pepper. Pour the egg mixture over the vegetables, then sprinkle the rosemary and thyme evenly over the top. Bake for 15 to 20 minutes, until the eggs are set, slightly puffed, and golden brown. A knife inserted into the center should come out clean. Cut into squares and serve hot or cold.

SLOW COOKER
Oatmeal

SERVES / 8

When my family relocates down the shore for the summer, I live in the kitchen. The house is always packed with people, I never know what time anyone is waking up, I'm always surprised by some new faces in the morning, and it's guaranteed everyone will be hungry. I throw this together right before I go to bed, and by the time I wake up, the kitchen smells incredible and a hot breakfast is ready and waiting. (As an added bonus, it actually lures people from their beds a little faster.) This recipe is a shore thing and a sure thing that stays warm all day and fills your belly.

2 cups [320 g] steel-cut oats

2 cups [280 g] dried cranberries

2 cups [320 g] dried figs, chopped (optional)

1 cup [240 ml] half-and-half

3 Tbsp unsalted butter

1 tsp dark brown sugar

In a slow cooker, stir together the oats, cranberries, figs (if using), half-and-half, butter, brown sugar, and 8 cups [1.9 L] of water. Cover and set on low heat for 8 to 10 hours. Stir well before serving.

LEFTOVER OATMEAL Bread

MAKES / 9 PIECES

This bread was also born down the shore, using the scrapings of whatever's left in the slow cooker from the Slow Cooker Oatmeal (facing page). When I'm on vacation, something takes over in the kitchen, a new sort of creativity kicks in, and my mind just goes places. This recipe is one of my experiments that really worked and has become a comforting tradition that's always around, and everyone knows it's coming when they see the oatmeal pot in the morning.

2 cups [280 g] all-purpose flour

1 tsp kosher salt

1/2 tsp baking soda

1/2 tsp baking powder

1/2 tsp ground cinnamon

1/2 tsp ground nutmeg

1/2 cup [113 g] unsalted butter, at room temperature

1/2 cup [100 g] granulated sugar

2 tsp vanilla extract

3 eggs

1/4 cup [60 ml] whole milk

1 cup [270 g] leftover oatmeal

1/2 cup [60 g] chopped walnuts

Decorative crystal sugar, for topping

Preheat the oven to 350°F [180°C]. Grease an 8 by 8 in [20 by 20 cm] baking pan.

In a large bowl, whisk together the flour, salt, baking soda, baking powder, cinnamon, and nutmeg.

In a medium bowl, use a handheld mixer at medium speed to cream together the butter, granulated sugar, and vanilla. Add the eggs one at a time, beating until each one is incorporated. Add half of the flour mixture and use a wooden spoon to combine. Stir in the milk, then the remaining flour mixture. Finally, fold in the oatmeal and walnuts.

Pour the batter into the prepared pan and sprinkle with decorative sugar. Bake for about 1 hour, until a knife inserted into the center comes out clean. Cool in the pan for about 30 minutes, then cut into nine pieces. Serve warm or at room temperature.

ZUCCHINI *Cake*

SERVES / 12

This cake was my last-ditch effort to get my kids to eat veggies when they were little. They flat-out refused to eat anything green, so this cake was just sneaky enough to trick them. The only problem is I could eat the entire cake myself. It's so moist and sweet and delicious, one of those things you keep sneaking back to all day for another tiny slice. My granddaughter, Markie, eats it now, as a new generation gets tricked into eating their vegetables.

1 cup [200 g] light brown sugar

½ cup [100 g] granulated sugar

½ cup [113 g] unsalted butter, at room temperature

½ cup [120 ml] extra-virgin olive oil

3 eggs

½ cup [120 ml] buttermilk

1 tsp vanilla extract

2½ cups [350 g] all-purpose flour

2 tsp baking soda

½ tsp ground allspice

½ tsp ground cinnamon

½ tsp kosher salt

2½ cups [325 g] grated zucchini (from about 2 medium zucchini)

Preheat the oven to 325°F [165°C]. Grease and flour a 9 by 13 in [23 by 33 cm] baking pan. Line with parchment paper, leaving 1 in [2.5 cm] of overhang.

In a large bowl, use a handheld mixer at medium speed to cream together the brown sugar, granulated sugar, butter, and olive oil. Add the eggs one at a time, beating until each one is incorporated. Beat in the buttermilk and vanilla. Sift in the flour, baking soda, allspice, cinnamon, and salt. Use a rubber spatula to fold until just a few streaks remain. Fold in the zucchini until combined.

Scrape into the prepared pan. Bake for 45 to 60 minutes, until a knife inserted into the center comes out clean. Cool completely in the pan, then use the parchment overhang to transfer the cake to a cutting board. Cut into twelve pieces and serve.

ZUCCHINI CAKE
PAGE 54

LEFTOVER
OATMEAL BREAD
PAGE 53

Classic FRENCH TOAST

SERVES / 4

My grandma and my mom made a lot of French toast when I was little. In a house of eleven hungry kids, it was quick, cheap, and an easy way to get us fed and shut us up. I think of them every time I'm dunking the bread to make this. It's the ultimate in classic comfort food, something that evokes warm memories of togetherness. And for me, it's an ode to the women who cared for me.

4 eggs

¼ cup [60 ml] whole milk

1 tsp vanilla extract

Kosher salt

Dash of ground cinnamon, plus more for serving

3 Tbsp unsalted butter

8 slices sandwich bread

¾ cup [255 g] pure maple syrup

In a medium shallow bowl, whisk the eggs, milk, vanilla, a good pinch of salt, and a dash of cinnamon until well blended.

On a griddle or in a large skillet over medium heat, melt 1 Tbsp of the butter. Working in batches, dip a slice of bread into the egg mixture, saturating both sides. Lay it on the griddle and keep dipping until the surface is full, but not crowded. Fry the bread until golden brown on each side, about 6 minutes total. Continue dipping and frying until all the bread is toasted.

Meanwhile, in a small saucepan over low heat, warm the maple syrup and remaining 2 Tbsp of butter, stirring occasionally to combine.

Divide the French toast among four plates and spoon the syrup mixture over the top. Serve with a sprinkle of cinnamon.

CRAB CAKE Benedict

SERVES / 2

This is a classic breakfast down the shore. One of our traditions every year is lobster night. Al goes out and buys a ridiculous amount of lobster and shellfish, and we cook it all and spread everything on the table outside. The next morning, I use any leftover crab to whip these up. I don't think I've ever made them at home, only when I can feel the salty breeze.

2 English muffins, split, toasted, and buttered

4 Crab Cakes (recipe follows)

4 eggs

Blender Hollandaise (recipe follows)

Divide the English muffin halves between two plates. Set a crab cake on each half.

In a large skillet over medium heat, heat 2 in [5 cm] of water until small bubbles just start to break the surface of the water. Working with one egg at a time, crack the egg into a small bowl. Lower the bowl to the surface of the water and tilt to slide the egg in. Repeat with the remaining eggs, leaving space between them. Simmer the eggs until the white is set and the yolk is runny, about 3 minutes.

Use a slotted spoon to remove each egg from the water. Blot the bottom of the spoon on paper towels to soak up excess water. Lay a poached egg on each crab cake. Spoon a heaping Tbsp of hollandaise over each egg and serve immediately.

CRAB CAKES

MAKES 12 CAKES

4 Tbsp [55 g] unsalted butter
1 celery stalk, minced
½ white onion, minced
Pinch of red pepper flakes
3 Tbsp all-purpose flour
½ tsp mustard powder
1 lb [455 g] fresh or canned lump crabmeat
1 cup [60 g] panko or crushed crackers
2 Tbsp fresh lemon juice
1 Tbsp mayonnaise
2 tsp kosher salt
1 tsp prepared horseradish

In a medium skillet over medium heat, melt 2 Tbsp of the butter. Add the celery, onion, and the red pepper flakes. Sauté until the onion is translucent, about 5 minutes. Stir in the flour and mustard powder and cook until thickened, about 2 minutes. Remove from the heat and stir in the crabmeat, panko, lemon juice, mayonnaise, salt, and horseradish.

Use a ¼ cup [60 ml] measure to scoop the mixture and flatten into patties. The patties can be fried right away or frozen for later. To freeze extra crab cakes, stack them in an airtight container with parchment between each patty. They can be frozen for up to 4 months.

When it's time to fry, in a large skillet over medium heat, melt the remaining 2 Tbsp of butter. Add the desired amount of patties and fry until golden brown on each side, about 8 minutes total. For frozen patties, make sure they're warmed all the way through and continue frying as needed.

BLENDER HOLLANDAISE

MAKES ⅓ CUP [80 ML]

1 egg yolk
2 tsp fresh lemon juice
¼ tsp kosher salt
Pinch of cayenne pepper
¼ cup [55 g] unsalted butter

Combine the egg yolk, lemon juice, salt, and cayenne in a blender. Pulse a couple of times to break the mix.

In a microwave-safe bowl, microwave the butter on high until just melted, 30 to 45 seconds. With the blender running, slowly pour in the melted butter in a stream to make a smooth and thick sauce. Use the hollandaise immediately.

Taylor Ham & CHEESE

SERVES / 1

---

1 Tbsp unsalted butter

1 egg

4 slices pork roll

2 slices American cheese

1 roll or bagel, split and toasted

Kosher salt and freshly ground black pepper

Ketchup, for serving (optional)

◆◆◆◆◆◆◆◆◆◆◆◆◆◆◆◆◆◆◆◆◆◆◆◆◆◆◆◆◆◆◆◆◆◆

This is arguably the signature dish of New Jersey, although we all can't seem to decide on a name. North Jersey calls it Taylor ham, South Jersey calls it pork roll (you can tell where my allegiances are). Whatever you call it, it's delicious. Before I had kids, this sandwich was my go-to diner order, the last stop after a late night out drinking, a kind of insurance policy against my hangover. After I had kids, when I was waking up at the same hour I used to be going to sleep, this became a comforting way to kick off the day. There's really no substitute for Taylor ham, but it can sometimes be tough to track down outside of New Jersey. Canadian bacon is a good swap for a different, but still delicious, sandwich!

◆◆◆◆◆◆◆◆◆◆◆◆◆◆◆◆◆◆◆◆◆◆◆◆◆◆◆◆◆◆◆◆◆◆

In a large nonstick skillet over medium heat, melt the butter. Crack the egg off to one side of the skillet and arrange the pork roll slices around the egg. Fry, flipping the pork roll halfway, until the egg is set and the pork roll is browned, about 3 minutes. Remove from the heat and lay a slice of cheese over the egg to soften.

On the bottom of the roll, lay two pieces of pork roll and the remaining slice of cheese. Lay the egg on top. Season with salt, pepper, and ketchup (if using). Layer on the remaining two slices of pork roll and the top of the roll. Serve hot.

N·O·T·E

This is optional, but if you cut a few slits around the perimeter of the pork roll, you get crispier edges!

Warm & Cozy

◆◆◆◆◆◆◆◆◆

My kitchen thrives in the fall and winter. I'm at my happiest when my table is full of the warm-to-your-core meals, house-filling aromas, and instant-classic dishes you crave. These are perfect when the temperature dips and you just want to linger around the table, all warm and cozy.

ESCAROLE & BEAN *Soup*

2 large heads escarole

¼ cup [60 ml] extra-virgin olive oil

6 garlic cloves, smashed

1 lb [455 g] hot or sweet Italian sausage, casings removed

Kosher salt

Red pepper flakes

Two 14.5 oz [410 g] cans chicken broth or 3½ cups [830 ml] chicken stock

One 15.5 oz [440 g] can cannellini beans

Parmesan rind (optional)

Parmesan cheese and crusty bread, for serving

My dad's mom made hearty soup every week, and this recipe has been a family favorite for generations. When I'm standing at the stove today, I feel like I'm eight years old again, watching Grandmom cook. It reminds me of her and I can feel her with me. Although every Italian family has their own version of this soup, everyone agrees on one rule: Don't even think about making it if you don't have bread ready to dip.

Rinse the escarole thoroughly in a strainer to make sure all the sand is out. Drain and roughly chop the escarole into 1 or 2 in [2.5 or 5 cm] pieces.

In a Dutch oven over medium heat, heat the olive oil. When the oil shimmers, add the garlic. Sauté until lightly browned, about 1 minute. Add the sausage and use a wooden spoon to break it up as it browns, about 5 minutes. Stir in the escarole and cover to let it wilt, about 2 minutes. Stir again to coat the escarole in the garlicky sausage fat. Season with a big pinch of salt and an up-to-you pinch of red pepper flakes.

Stir in the broth and beans. (If you have a rind of Parmesan, throw in a 1 in [2.5 cm] chunk! But the soup will still be great without it.) Cover and simmer until the flavors meld, about 20 minutes. Taste for seasoning. Remove and discard the rind (if using).

Ladle into bowls and serve with Parmesan for grating and plenty of bread for dipping.

ITALIAN
WEDDING SOUP
PAGE 66

ESCAROLE &
BEAN SOUP
PAGE 64

ITALIAN WEDDING *Soup*

SERVES / 8

2 qt [1.9 L] chicken stock

1 large carrot, diced

1 celery stalk, diced

Kosher salt and freshly ground black pepper

Parmesan rind (optional)

¼ cup [50 g] orzo or acini de pepe pasta

1 lb [455 g] Meatball mix (page 139 or 142)

2 cups [40 g] baby spinach, chopped

Parmesan cheese and crusty bread, for serving

This warm-you-from-the-inside soup is reserved for the coldest, snowiest of days, when I know I'm not going anywhere. It's a simple soup, requiring no special trips to the grocery. But every one of these humble ingredients plays its part to create a soup filled with a lot of comforting flavors.

In a large pot, combine the chicken stock, carrot, celery, and a couple big pinches of salt and pepper. (If you have a rind of Parmesan, throw in a 1 in [2.5 cm] chunk!) Set over high heat and bring to a boil. Add the pasta and cook until al dente according to the package directions.

Turn the heat to low. Use a 1 Tbsp measure to scoop the meatball mix and add to the soup. Simmer until the meatballs are cooked through, about 10 minutes. Stir in the spinach to wilt, about 30 seconds, then remove from the heat. Remove and discard the rind (if using).

Ladle the soup into bowls and serve with Parmesan for grating and plenty of bread for dipping.

Vegetarian STUFFED PEPPERS

SERVES / 8

I used to make the traditional style of stuffed peppers, the kind where you slice the top off and stuff the whole pepper. But my mother-in-law always made them this way—let's call them open-faced peppers—and I loved them. It's a really beautiful presentation, being able to see the stuffing and the vibrant pepper underneath. These are great as a side dish or a vegetarian main. A hearty and healthy mix of veggies, plus a good amount of cheese, feels really comforting, especially in the fall and winter. Even though this recipe serves eight, I like to make a batch for Al and me to eat throughout the week because the flavors get better the longer they sit.

½ cup [113 g] unsalted butter

1 white onion, diced

2 garlic cloves, minced

1 medium zucchini, diced

1 small eggplant, diced

2 portobello mushrooms, diced

Kosher salt and freshly ground black pepper

1½ cups [360 ml] vegetable broth

½ cup [120 ml] dry white wine

2 Tbsp finely chopped fresh basil

1 Tbsp fresh thyme leaves

4 slices white bread, crusts removed, cut into 1 in [2.5 cm] cubes

1 cup [140 g] seasoned bread crumbs

1 cup [80 g] shredded low-moisture mozzarella

½ cup [30 g] grated pecorino or ½ cup [15 g] Parmesan cheese

4 red bell peppers

Preheat the oven to 350°F [180°C].

In a large skillet over medium heat, melt ¼ cup [55 g] of the butter. Add the onion and garlic and sauté until translucent and very fragrant, about 5 minutes. Add the zucchini, eggplant, mushrooms, and a big pinch of salt and pepper. Sauté, stirring occasionally, until the vegetables release their liquid and it cooks off, about 10 minutes. Stir in ½ cup [120 ml] of the broth, the wine, the basil, and the thyme. Once the mixture comes to a simmer, remove from the heat. Stir in the bread cubes, bread crumbs, mozzarella, and pecorino.

Slice the bell peppers in half vertically, to create eight long halves. Discard the seeds. Arrange the halves in a 9 by 13 in [23 by 33 cm] baking pan. Divide the mixture evenly among the peppers. Cut the remaining ¼ cup [55 g] of butter into eight pieces and place one piece on top of the stuffing in each pepper. Pour the remaining 1 cup [240 ml] of broth into the pan.

Cover the pan with aluminum foil and bake for 30 minutes, until the peppers are nicely soft. Increase the temperature to 400°F [200°C] and remove the foil. Bake for 10 to 15 minutes, until the stuffing is nicely browned. Serve immediately.

Penne WITH VODKA SAUCE

SERVES / 6 TO 8

This was a favorite when my kids were little and now my granddaughter, Markie, asks for the "orange pasta" when she comes over. I like to make it with a mix of canned and fresh tomatoes for texture, and I add peas, because having them covered in a healthy dose of delicious, savory sauce was the only way my kids would eat their veggies. Personally, I like the bright green against the pink sauce, so it's just become part of the dish. My oldest son, Albie, to this day still loves penne with vodka and loves when I have it ready and waiting for him.

4 Tbsp [55 g] unsalted butter

1 small white onion, diced

2 garlic cloves, minced

4 oz [115 g] thinly sliced prosciutto or pancetta, cut into strips

½ tsp red pepper flakes

One 28 oz [795 g] can crushed tomatoes

½ cup [120 ml] chicken stock

¼ cup [60 ml] vodka

½ tsp kosher salt

½ cup [120 ml] heavy cream

½ cup [30 g] grated pecorino cheese, plus more for serving

4 plum tomatoes, diced

One 10 oz [285 g] bag frozen peas

1 lb [455 g] dried penne

In a large pot over medium heat, melt the butter. Add the onion and garlic and sauté, stirring often, until the onion is translucent, about 3 minutes. Stir in the prosciutto and sauté until crisp, about 2 minutes. Stir in the red pepper flakes and cook until fragrant, about 30 seconds.

Stir in the crushed tomatoes, chicken stock, vodka, and salt. Simmer until the liquid has reduced, about 20 minutes. Stir in the cream, pecorino, diced tomatoes, and peas. Simmer for about 5 minutes until the sauce is nice and thick.

While the sauce is simmering, bring a large pot of salted water to a boil over high heat. Cook the penne to al dente according to the package directions. Drain the pasta and add to the sauce off the heat. Stir until the pasta is completely coated in the sauce. Serve with more pecorino for sprinkling.

N·O·T·E

Don't microwave leftover pasta! Add it to a skillet with a splash of water, set over medium heat, and toss until warmed through.

Creamy BROCCOLI CAVATELLI

SERVES / 4 TO 6

1 head broccoli, cut into bite-size florets

¼ cup [60 ml] extra-virgin olive oil

5 garlic cloves, smashed

2 cups [480 ml] chicken stock

Kosher salt and freshly ground black pepper

1 lb [455 g] dried cavatelli

Juice of 1 lemon

Red pepper flakes

Grated pecorino cheese

My grandparents on both sides of my family made this, my mom and dad made it, basically everyone in my family made it. So it's no surprise it's one of my favorite dishes ever. It's a breeze to make and packed with so much flavor. Every time I smell the garlic and broccoli hit the hot oil, it reminds me of my childhood. I recommend doubling up the recipe when you make it because it reheats so well and the flavors get better every day.

Bring a large pot of salted water to a boil over high heat. Stir in the broccoli and boil until vibrant green, about 2 minutes. Use a spider strainer or slotted spoon to remove the broccoli to a colander. Keep the pot of boiling water for the pasta later.

In a large saucepan over medium heat, heat the olive oil. When the oil shimmers, add the garlic and sauté until lightly golden, about 2 minutes. Stir in the broccoli and sauté until covered in garlic flavor, about 2 more minutes. Add the chicken stock and a good pinch of salt and pepper. Simmer until the stock is reduced by half, about 10 minutes.

Meanwhile, stir the cavatelli into the pot of boiling water. Cook to al dente according to the package directions. Drain the pasta, then add it to the broccoli mixture off the heat. Squeeze the lemon juice into the saucepan. Add a pinch of red pepper flakes and a big handful of pecorino. Stir until everything is thoroughly combined. Serve with more pecorino for sprinkling.

Don't microwave leftover pasta! Add it to a skillet with a splash of water, set over medium heat, and toss until warmed through.

Cheesy BROCCOLI RABE & WHITE BEAN Pasta

SERVES / 6 TO 8

1 lb [455 g] broccoli rabe

2 Tbsp extra-virgin olive oil

1 lb [455 g] hot or sweet Italian sausage, casings removed

½ cup [115 g] diced pancetta

6 garlic cloves, smashed

½ tsp red pepper flakes

Kosher salt and freshly ground black pepper

One 15.5 oz [440 g] can cannellini beans, rinsed and drained

1 cup [240 ml] chicken stock

1 lb [455 g] dried orecchiette

2 Tbsp finely chopped fresh parsley

¼ cup [15 g] grated pecorino cheese

This is one of my go-to weeknight dinners, especially when I'm looking for something last-minute. The ingredient list is basically a list of things I keep in stock at all times. Seriously, check page 27 if you don't believe me. I just swap out whatever pasta I have at the moment. Every Italian has broccoli rabe or broccolini in the fridge at all times; it's a law. But this is also a good excuse to chop up and save any dying greens you have around.

N·O·T·E

Don't microwave leftover pasta! Add it to a skillet with a splash of water, set over medium heat, and toss until warmed through.

Rinse the broccoli rabe thoroughly under cold running water and drain well. Trim off the bottom 1 in [2.5 cm] or so of the stems, plus the lower leaves. Chop the stems and leaves into 2 in [5 cm] pieces.

In a large skillet over medium heat, heat the olive oil. When the oil shimmers, add the sausage and pancetta. Use a wooden spoon to break up the sausage as it browns, about 5 minutes. Add the garlic and red pepper flakes and stir until fragrant, about 2 minutes.

Add the broccoli rabe with a good pinch of salt and pepper. Cover the skillet and turn the heat to low. Let the broccoli rabe steam until crisp-tender, about 10 minutes. Add the cannellini beans and chicken stock. Let the mixture simmer, stirring occasionally, until the liquid is reduced by half, about 10 minutes.

Meanwhile, bring a large pot of salted water to a boil over high heat. Cook the orecchiette to al dente according to the package directions. Drain the pasta, then add it back to the same pot off the heat. Scrape the broccoli rabe mixture into the pot and stir to thoroughly coat the pasta. Stir in the parsley and pecorino. Taste for seasoning and serve hot.

COOK for a CROWD

Cooking for a crowd? Expect the unexpected!

When I'm hosting, I know at least half a dozen unplanned guests will stroll in. I know someone will wait until they arrive to tell me they went vegan last week. And I know everyone is coming ready to eat and the hangry clock is ticking. Stretching food and thinking on my feet is my normal. After some big crash-and-burns, I've figured out my top five ways to save the day without breaking a sweat:

1 **BE READY.** Have a good arsenal in the pantry (see page 27) to improvise or add to what you're already making. It doesn't have to be overly stocked, but just the basic building blocks to pull together a simple soup or pasta. Next time you're shopping for the basics, throw a couple extra in your cart for backup. I use the same philosophy with my freezer. If I'm making lasagna, I'll make two and freeze one. Sauce on the stove? Double it and tuck the extra away. I'll tell you what, thawing is a lot faster than starting from scratch.

2 **EMBRACE SIMPLICITY.** If I'm in the middle of roasting a chicken and five new people walk in, there's no way I'm running out to get a second chicken. I just look for the easiest solution to bulk up everything around the chicken. Can I throw together a pasta to serve alongside? Do I have a ball of dough to make a pizza? What's in the fridge that can become a salad? There are a lot of simple answers that don't compromise on flavor or filling the table with great food.

3 **SNACK ATTACK.** If you're short on the main, load them up on appetizers. Grab every cheese, cured meat, dried fruit, raw vegetable, chip, dip, and carb in sight. Almost anything is delicious served on crostini, and an improvised pizza can be cut into tiny pieces. Arrange everything on a large board or in small bowls, and let the snacking begin!

4 **CREATE STATIONS.** If the people outnumber the chairs, it's time to switch tactics. Make the meal a free-flowing event, kind of like a cocktail party, but with bigger portions. Set out the meal buffet style or arrange each dish in different areas so everyone can move and mingle while they eat. Just keep the alcohol flowing and everyone will feel like it was the best dinner party ever.

5 **GO BIG.** If I'm cooking for ten, I'm cooking for twenty because I want everyone to leave full, happy, and with a container of leftovers. By embracing a mentality of abundance, I've saved my butt on more than one occasion. The best part about Italian American cooking is that almost everything keeps overnight and almost everything tastes better the next day. So I get a head start a day or two before and work in big batches.

Star SOUP

SERVES / 2

Star soup was my mom's signature soup. She would send us out to play in the snow and have this and an English Muffin Pizza (page 209) waiting when we got inside. When I was sick, it was guaranteed that I'd get a mug of this to warm me up. When my kids were little, I continued the star soup tradition, and now my daughter makes it for her daughter. It's so simple, but impossible not to love. Even though my kids are grown up, it's still one of their favorite things. Albie is a grated cheese addict, so he always adds a pile to his soup; Lauren and Christopher like it as is!

8 oz [230 g] dried pastina

One 14.5 oz [410 g] can chicken stock

Kosher salt and freshly ground black pepper

Grated Parmesan cheese, for serving (optional)

Bring a medium saucepan filled with salted water to a boil over high heat. Cook the pastina to al dente according to the package directions. Drain the pasta, then return it to the same saucepan. Add the stock and a good pinch of salt and pepper. Heat until the stock just starts to simmer. Serve with grated Parmesan, if desired. Done! I told you it was easy!

SPAGHETTI
WITH
Crab Sauce

SERVES / 8

This is a perfect meal to feed a crowd any time—winter, spring, summer, or fall. Crabmeat has such a natural, subtle sweetness that works perfectly with al dente spaghetti and this wine sauce. I've also made this with lobster, shrimp, and scallops when good crabmeat isn't available. It's a simple dish that feels just special enough, filling but not too rich, celebratory but not specific. It'll just make everyone feel warm and cozy.

1 lb [455 g] dried spaghetti

2 Tbsp extra-virgin olive oil, plus more for serving

6 garlic cloves, minced

½ tsp red pepper flakes

1 cup [240 ml] chicken stock

½ cup [120 ml] dry white wine

Kosher salt and freshly ground black pepper

1 lb [455 g] fresh or canned lump crabmeat

3 Tbsp finely chopped fresh parsley

Juice of ½ lemon

Grated pecorino cheese, for garnish

Bring a large pot of salted water to a boil over high heat. Cook the spaghetti to al dente according to the package directions. Reserve ½ cup [120 ml] of the pasta water, then drain the pasta.

While the pasta cooks, heat the olive oil in a large skillet over medium heat. When the oil shimmers, add the garlic and red pepper flakes. Sauté until lightly browned, about 1 minute. Add the chicken stock, white wine, and a small pinch of salt and pepper. Simmer until the liquid reduces by half, about 6 minutes. Add the crabmeat and stir to coat in the liquid. Cook until the crab is a vibrant pink, about 3 minutes.

Add the pasta and ¼ cup [60 ml] of the reserved pasta water. Simmer, tossing constantly to coat the pasta in the sauce, until the crab is cooked through and the sauce is nicely thick, about 2 more minutes. Add the parsley and lemon juice and toss. Add a splash more of the remaining pasta water as needed. Taste for seasoning.

Transfer the pasta to a large serving plate. Drizzle with some more olive oil and garnish with a few sprinkles of pecorino before serving.

N·O·T·E

Don't microwave leftover pasta! Add it to a skillet with a splash of water, set over medium heat, and toss until warmed through.

TURKEY & VEGETABLE
Meatloaf

SERVES / 8

I love meatloaf and will happily eat it any time of day. I will eat it in a sandwich, as a late night snack, with a fried egg for breakfast. There's never a wrong time. This version, made with turkey, is maybe my favorite version I've ever made. Turkey meat is more delicate than beef, so it really lets the other flavors jump out, like lots of vegetables and fragrant herbs.

1 medium carrot, shredded

1 medium zucchini, diced

1 bell pepper, diced

2 cups [40 g] spinach, chopped

4 Tbsp [55 g] unsalted butter

1 medium white onion, diced

1 garlic clove, minced

1 medium vine tomato, chopped

1 Tbsp finely chopped fresh parsley

1 Tbsp finely chopped fresh chives

1 Tbsp finely chopped fresh tarragon

1 egg

2 slices white sandwich bread

2 lb [910 g] lean ground turkey

Kosher salt and freshly ground black pepper

½ cup [170 g] ketchup

Preheat the oven to 375°F [190°C]. Line a 5 by 9 in [13 by 23 cm] loaf pan with parchment paper, leaving 1 in [2.5 cm] of overhang on the sides.

In a food processor, combine half each of the carrot, zucchini, bell pepper, and spinach. Pulse about ten times to form a thick paste.

In a large skillet over medium heat, melt the butter. Add the onion and garlic and sauté until the onion is translucent, about 5 minutes. Add the vegetable paste to the skillet and cook until fragrant, about 1 minute. Add the remaining carrot, zucchini, bell pepper, and spinach, plus the tomato, parsley, chives, and tarragon. Sauté, stirring often, until the vegetables release their liquid and it cooks off, about 15 minutes.

Meanwhile, in the same food processor, combine the egg, white bread, and 2 Tbsp of water. Pulse about four times until combined. Scrape the mixture into a large bowl. Add the turkey with a big pinch of salt and pepper. Use your hands to mix until combined, being careful not to overwork the meat.

Add the vegetable mixture to the bowl and fold to combine. Scrape into the prepared loaf pan and smooth into an even layer. Brush the ketchup evenly over the top.

Bake for 45 to 60 minutes, until golden brown and cooked through (an internal temperature of 170°F [77°C]). Let cool for 20 minutes in the pan, then use the parchment to transfer the loaf to a cutting board. Cut into eight pieces and serve immediately.

Easy TURKEY CHILI

1 Tbsp extra-virgin olive oil

1 lb [455 g] ground turkey

5 plum tomatoes, diced

1 green bell pepper, diced

1 medium white onion, diced

5 garlic cloves, minced

Kosher salt

1 tsp chili powder

½ tsp smoked paprika

½ tsp dried oregano

½ tsp red pepper flakes

¼ tsp cayenne pepper

Two 8 oz [230 g] cans tomato sauce

One 15.5 oz [440 g] can cannellini beans, rinsed and drained

One 4 oz [115 g] can diced green chiles, with liquid

Sour cream, shredded Cheddar cheese, and tortilla chips, for serving

When you don't have a lot of time or don't feel like cooking, you make chili. I don't make the rules, I just live by them. I do like my chili a little spicy, and yes, I've been known to break the chili law and add beans. This recipe is just a base, but I can guarantee I've never made a chili the same way twice, so go ahead and play with the ingredients as you like. It's always going to be filling, satisfying, and just as good four days later.

In a Dutch oven over medium heat, heat the olive oil. When the oil shimmers, add the turkey and use a wooden spoon to break it up as it browns, about 5 minutes. Add the tomatoes, bell pepper, onion, garlic, and a big pinch of salt. Continue cooking, stirring often, until the vegetables are softened, about 5 more minutes. Stir in the chili powder, paprika, oregano, red pepper flakes, and cayenne and cook until fragrant, about 1 minute. Add the tomato sauce, cannellini beans, green chiles with the liquid, and another big pinch of salt. Stir well to combine, turn the heat to low, and simmer for 1 hour, stirring occasionally.

Divide the chili among bowls. Garnish with sour cream and Cheddar cheese and don't forget the chips on the side!

N·O·T·E

This chili is lightly spicy, but adjust the red pepper flakes and cayenne to your liking. More for hot, less for mild!

CRISPY BROILED
Chicken Thighs

SERVES / 4 TO 8

---

8 bone-in, skin-on chicken thighs

½ cup [120 ml] extra-virgin olive oil

Juice of 1 lemon

4 garlic cloves, thinly sliced

2 Tbsp finely chopped fresh parsley

1 Tbsp dried oregano

2 tsp kosher salt, plus more as needed

1 tsp freshly ground black pepper, plus more as needed

½ tsp red pepper flakes

2 red onions, halved and sliced

8 Italian long hots, raw or marinated

Crusty bread or Garlic Bread (page 41), for serving

Growing up, my grandmother would make broiled chicken a lot. Her recipe was very simple, just an easy marinade of pantry staples and a quick broil over some vegetables. But its simplicity is what made it so good: perfectly juicy chicken thighs with perfectly crisp skin. Sometimes letting the ingredient sing is the best answer, and this is a dish that *really* sings. For my take on her recipe, I like to use a mix of red onions and red hots, which get soaked in all the great chicken fat dripping from the thighs. Sopping up the pan juices with bread is almost better than the main event, so make sure you have lots of bread on the table. This recipe will feed the family or make a batch for two with the leftovers lying around to adapt into other dishes.

In a large zip-top bag, combine the chicken thighs, olive oil, lemon juice, garlic, parsley, oregano, salt, black pepper, and red pepper flakes. Seal the bag tightly and shake to mix the marinade and coat the chicken. Set in the refrigerator overnight to marinate. About 30 minutes before baking, remove the chicken from the refrigerator to come to room temperature.

Set the broiler to high.

In a 9 by 13 in [23 by 33 cm] baking dish, toss the onions, long hots, and ¼ cup [60 ml] of the marinade. Spread out the veggies evenly. Remove the chicken from the marinade and arrange skin-side down over the veggies. Pour the remaining marinade over the chicken. Slide the baking dish under the broiler and broil for 10 minutes, rotating the baking dish halfway through. Remove the baking dish and flip the chicken skin-side up. Broil again for about 15 more minutes, rotating the dish halfway through, until the chicken skin is crisp and the thighs reach at least 170°F [77°C] on a meat thermometer. Serve immediately with plenty of bread for sopping up the pan juices.

WFC

{WHOLE F**KING CHICKEN}

(SERVES / 8)

One 6 lb [2.7 kg] roasting chicken

Kosher salt and freshly ground black pepper

2 bunches herbs (see Note)

Fruit (see Note)

1 white onion, halved

1 garlic bulb, halved

¼ cup [60 ml] extra-virgin olive oil

1 cup [240 ml] chicken stock

◆◆◆◆◆◆◆◆◆◆◆◆◆◆◆◆◆◆◆◆◆◆◆

When you're up against a group of people with a lot of opinions, the worst question is, "What should we make?" At some point, I gave up on catering to everyone's individual wants and needs and I said, "Screw it, let's make a whole fucking chicken." The name stuck and now my family calls it WFC for short. The great thing is the flavors are totally adaptable to the seasons. In the fall I grab heartier herbs and stuff the chicken with apples and pears. In the summer, I do more delicate herbs and use citrus in the cavity. Either way, the prep work is simple and then the whole thing goes in the oven, easy. For the days when you feel like you just can't win, here's a whole fucking chicken.

◆◆◆◆◆◆◆◆◆◆◆◆◆◆◆◆◆◆◆◆◆◆◆

Preheat the oven to 425°F [220°C].

Remove any giblets from the chicken and rinse the cavity. Use paper towels to pat the chicken dry, inside and out. Heavily season the inside of the chicken with good pinches of salt and pepper. Stuff the cavity with the herbs, fruit, onion, and garlic.

Brush the entire outside of the chicken with the olive oil, then season heavily with a few pinches of salt and pepper. Tuck the wing tips under the body. Set the chicken in a roasting pan and add the stock to the pan. Roast the chicken for 1½ hours, until the breast reaches at least 160°F [71°C] and the thigh reaches at least 170°F [77°C] on a meat thermometer. Baste the chicken with the pan juices, then transfer to a cutting board. Loosely cover the chicken with aluminum foil and let it rest for 15 minutes before carving and serving.

 For the herbs, I like to use thyme, rosemary, and sage in colder months and basil, tarragon, and parsley in warmer months. For the fruit, I like to quarter 1 apple and 1 pear when it's chilly, and when it's hot I do thin slices of 1 navel orange and 1 lemon.

Pork Chops,
POTATOES & VINEGAR PEPPERS

8 medium Yukon gold
  potatoes

Four to six 1 in [2.5 cm] thick
  center-cut pork chops,
  bone-in or boneless

Kosher salt and freshly
  ground black pepper

1 cup [240 ml] whole milk

½ cup [70 g] all-purpose flour

½ cup [70 g] bread crumbs

¼ cup [60 ml] canola oil

1 large white onion, halved
  and sliced

One 12 oz [340 g] jar sliced
  vinegar peppers

Sunday dinner at my house
is *not* a drive-by situation. If
you're here, you're committing
to spending serious time at the
table. (Or if it's an especially
crowded Sunday, grabbing a
plate and squeezing onto any
couch you can find.) This recipe
for pork and roasted veggies is
a favorite of mine because, after
a little prep, all the real work
happens in the oven, giving me
time to eat. By the time we're
finished with the pasta course,
our main course is ready to come
out of the oven. And trust me,
even when you think you can't
eat any more, the aroma of the
pork and peppers will reignite
any appetite. It's always been a
favorite of my son Christopher,
and I think it'll be yours too.

Preheat the oven to 350°F [180°C].

Bring a large pot of salted water to a boil over high heat. While
waiting for the water to boil, peel and cube the potatoes. Add
to the water and boil until fork-tender, 10 to 12 minutes. Drain
and set aside.

Rinse the pork chops and pat dry with paper towels. Season well
with salt and pepper.

In a medium shallow bowl, add the milk. Whisk the flour and
bread crumbs in a separate medium shallow bowl. Working one
at a time, coat a pork chop in the milk and let the excess drip
off. Dredge the chop in the flour mixture, pressing to make sure
it's completely coated. Set aside on a plate while dredging the
remaining chops.

In a large oven-safe skillet over medium heat, heat the canola oil.
When the oil shimmers, add the onion with a good pinch of salt
and pepper. Cook, stirring occasionally, until the onion just starts
to soften, about 3 minutes. Nestle the dredged pork chops in
the skillet and sear for about 4 minutes on each side. (You're not
cooking them through, just enough to get both sides golden
brown.) Remove the skillet from the heat.

Add the potatoes and jar of peppers (liquid and all!) to the same
skillet. Toss to mix everything together and season as needed.

Bake for 25 to 30 minutes, until the veggies are nicely browned
and the pork reaches at least 160°F [71°C] on a meat thermometer.

Serve immediately or loosely tent the pan with aluminum foil for
up to 15 minutes before serving.

N·O·T·E

I prefer Cento for
my peppers, but any
brand will work!

Deep-Dish SAUSAGE PIZZA PIE

SERVES / 8

This was a mistake that worked. I am not good at making pizza—the dough and I do not get along. Some people have the magic touch and can coax a perfect pie out of thin air (literally). But me, I can never make a round shape, the dough tears, it sticks all over the counter, and I end up serving an amoeba-shaped pizza. So I gave up and made a pie. It hits the spot just like pizza and comes out beautifully, no matter how terribly you rolled your dough!

2 lb [910 g] pizza dough

2 Tbsp extra-virgin olive oil

1 large white onion, diced

4 garlic cloves, minced

1 lb [455 g] hot or sweet Italian sausage, casings removed

One 8 oz [230 g] can tomato sauce

Kosher salt and freshly ground black pepper

2 cups [160 g] shredded mozzarella cheese

½ cup [30 g] grated pecorino cheese

Set a rack in the lower third of the oven. Preheat the oven to 350°F [180°C]. Grease a deep-dish pie plate or 8 in [20 cm] cake pan.

Cut the pizza dough in half. On a floured work surface, roll out one half of the dough to a rough 13 in [33 cm] circle. Transfer the dough to the prepared pie plate, lifting and pressing to ease the dough into the corners and leaving about 1 in [2.5 cm] of overhang. Transfer the pie plate to the refrigerator to chill while making the filling. Cover the other half of the dough with plastic wrap and set aside.

In a large skillet over medium heat, heat the olive oil. When the oil shimmers, add the onion and garlic. Sauté until translucent, about 5 minutes. Add the sausage and use a wooden spoon to break it up as it browns, about 5 minutes. Stir in the tomato sauce and season with a good pinch of salt and pepper. Remove from the heat and let cool for 30 minutes.

Roll the remaining half of the dough into a rough 10 in [25 cm] circle and keep it on standby. Remove the pie plate from the fridge. Sprinkle ½ cup [40 g] of the mozzarella and ¼ cup [15 g] of the pecorino over the bottom of the crust. Spoon half of the sausage sauce into the pie. Cover with 1 cup [80 g] of the mozzarella, then spoon the remaining sauce over the top to fill the plate. Finish with the remaining ½ cup [40 g] of mozzarella and ¼ cup [15 g] of pecorino, then lay the remaining half of dough on top. Roll the overhanging dough into a tight crust around the perimeter.

Transfer to the lower rack and bake for about 45 minutes, until the crust is deeply golden brown. Remove from the oven and let rest for about 20 minutes before slicing and serving.

Al Fresco

• • • • ◆ ◆ ◆ ◆ ◆ ◆ ◆

In warmer weather, when sweating
over a stove is out of the question, the party
moves outside for a generous helping of fresh air.
These are my favorite grill-ready or make-ahead
starters, sides, and mains that just taste better
when enjoyed al fresco!

DOWN THE SHORE

Smothered CORN COBS

SERVES / 8

SMOTHER

½ cup [113 g] unsalted butter, at room temperature

½ cup [15 g] grated Parmesan cheese

1 tsp garlic salt

1 tsp dried oregano

½ tsp red pepper flakes

COBS

½ cup [120 ml] whole milk

4 Tbsp [55 g] unsalted butter

1 Tbsp kosher salt

8 ears of corn, shucked

Summertime in New Jersey means corn on the cob. When we're at the shore house, we're eating it almost every night. But even the sweetest and juiciest ear can use a little more than just salt and butter. I always try to make food fun and delicious, so over the years I've played with all sorts of ways to dress up the corn. After some highs and lows, I finally nailed down my dream corn. A beautifully smothered ear of corn totally changes the narrative of what a grilled corn cob can be.

TO MAKE THE SMOTHER: In a small bowl, whisk together the butter, Parmesan, garlic salt, oregano, and red pepper flakes. Store at room temperature until ready to use.

TO MAKE THE COBS: Bring a large pot with 4 qt [3.8 L] of water to a boil over high heat. Stir in the milk, butter, and salt. Once the butter is melted, lower in the corn. (Or work in batches if all the cobs won't fit.) Boil for 3 to 5 minutes, until the corn is vibrant and tender. Remove the corn to cool.

Prepare the grill for medium-high heat (about 400°F [200°C]). Grill the corn, turning often, until charred on all sides and cooked through, 8 to 10 minutes total. Cradle the cobs in pieces of foil and immediately cover with the smother. Serve in the foil packets so all that good butter doesn't go to waste.

 **If you're grilling for a crowd, just multiply the smother. The milky corn water can be used for as many batches of corn as you need; just keep them flowing in and out.**

Easy GRILLED POTATO PACKETS

Russet or Yukon gold
  potatoes

Thinly sliced white onion

Kosher salt and freshly
  ground black pepper

Unsalted butter

Fresh rosemary sprigs

SERVES / AS MANY AS YOU WANT

There are only two rules for this classic no-recipe recipe: One, figure about one large potato per person, and two, seal your foil packets tightly. That's it! My mom used to make this as an easy side for eleven hungry kids, and we loved it because we each got to open our own little present. Now it's become my go-to all summer because it's easy to make on the fly and you can just throw the packets on the grill while everything else cooks. Even easier: They can be made ahead and sit at room temperature or in the refrigerator until it's time to grill. Seasonings are up to you, but I like this classic mix of butter, rosemary, and a little onion.

Tear a piece of heavy-duty aluminum foil that's about 12 in [30.5 cm] long. Drizzle some olive oil on the surface of the foil.

Scrub and thinly slice the potatoes (no need to peel, unless you want to). Spread the onion slices on the foil, then pile the potatoes on top. Season with a good pinch of salt and pepper, then add a couple pats of butter. Nestle a rosemary sprig in there.

This is the crucial step. Bring the edges of the foil together, leaving headroom for steam to build. Fold the seams down, then fold a second time to ensure the packet is completely sealed.

Prepare the grill for medium-high heat (about 450°F [230°C]). Arrange the packets on the grates. Cover and grill, rotating the packets occasionally so they cook evenly. After 30 to 40 minutes, when the potatoes are tender, remove from the grill. Open carefully (lots of hot steam in there!) and serve immediately.

NOTE

If you don't have heavy-duty foil, stack two sheets of regular foil. You'll want an extra layer of protection so the potatoes don't burn before they steam.

Grilled ARTICHOKES
WITH LEMON AIOLI

SERVES / 3 TO 6

◆◆◆◆◆◆◆◆◆◆◆◆◆◆◆◆◆◆◆◆◆◆◆◆◆

This is a perfect appetizer on its own or as part of an Antipasti Spread (page 153). I like to get all my artichoke prep done the night before (it's not hard, it just takes some work) so when it's time to get cooking, I can throw batches on the grill and keep them coming. The lemon aioli is a perfect partner for this—really delicious and light.

◆◆◆◆◆◆◆◆◆◆◆◆◆◆◆◆◆◆◆◆◆◆◆◆

3 large globe artichokes

1 lemon, halved

Extra-virgin olive oil, for brushing

Kosher salt and freshly ground black pepper

Lemon Aioli (page 34), for serving

Fill a large pot halfway with salted water. Set over high heat and bring to a boil while you trim the artichokes.

You'll need a paring knife, chef's knife, kitchen scissors, and the halved lemon nearby. Use the paring knife to trim off the very bottom of the artichoke stem. Rub with lemon. Carefully shave off the tough outer layer of the stem with the paring knife. Rub lemon all over the cut stem. Using the scissors, snip off the pointy tips of the leaves, until you get to the top, where the leaves are too crowded to separate. Rub the lemon over the outside of the artichoke so the cut parts don't brown. Lay the artichoke on a cutting board and use the chef's knife to slice the artichoke in half lengthwise from top to stem. Rub each exposed inner half all over with lemon. Cut about ¾ in [2 cm] off at the tip of each half, removing the last bunch of pointy tips. Rub the exposed ends with lemon. Repeat with the other two artichokes.

Lower the cut artichokes into the boiling water. Set a heatproof bowl over the artichokes to keep them submerged. Cook the artichokes until a paring knife easily pierces them, about 20 minutes. Use tongs to remove the bowl, then transfer the artichoke halves, cut-side down, to paper towels. Once they've dried off, transfer them to a plate and cover in plastic wrap. Refrigerate for 1 hour to cool, or overnight if you're prepping ahead.

Before grilling, use a small spoon to scoop the chokes (the hairy part near the heart) out of the cooled artichokes. If they chilled overnight, let them sit at room temperature for 30 minutes.

Prepare the grill for medium-high heat (about 450°F [230°C]). Brush the artichokes generously on both sides with olive oil and season all over with a few good pinches of salt and pepper. Grill the artichokes, outside first then cut side, until nicely charred, about 5 minutes per side. Arrange the artichokes on a serving platter. Drizzle with olive oil and season with a little more pepper. Serve hot with the lemon aioli for dipping.

Smoky GRILLED PEACHES

SERVES / 6

6 very ripe peaches

½ cup [120 ml] extra-virgin olive oil, plus more for the grill

¼ cup [60 ml] balsamic vinegar

12 Tbsp [150 g] light brown sugar

Toasted chopped hazelnuts (optional), for serving

Grilled peaches are the peak of summer. And my magic trick for perfectly grilled fruit is lining the grill with foil so the peaches can char without getting stuck. Once they're smoky and warm, I like to put these on a pizza, in a salad, or alongside prosciutto—the possibilities are endless. But my favorite way to use these peaches is as a simple dessert served hot with a scoop of melting ice cream. It's heaven!

Line the grill grates with aluminum foil. Prepare the grill for medium-high heat (about 450°F [230°C]).

Halve and pit the peaches. Rub them all over with the olive oil and arrange on a large plate, cut-side up. Drizzle the balsamic vinegar all over the cut sides. Let them sit at room temperature for 30 minutes to marinate.

Just before grilling, brush the foil with plenty of olive oil. This will ensure the peaches char without getting stuck. Lay the peaches cut-side down on the foil and grill for about 5 minutes, until nicely charred. Flip the peaches and add 1 Tbsp of the brown sugar on each cut side. Close the lid and grill for about 3 minutes, until the brown sugar melts into the peaches.

Divide the peaches among six bowls and serve with a sprinkling of hazelnuts (if using).

If you serve the peaches with ice cream, vanilla is classic, but I also love using coconut or pistachio.

SUMMER Caprese Salad

◆◆◆◆◆◆◆◆◆◆◆◆◆◆◆◆◆◆◆◆◆◆◆◆◆◆◆◆◆◆◆◆

This is a starting point for caprese, a perfect amount for two people. But honestly, how many times in my life do you think I've made anything that serves two? I'm constantly multiplying this to feed a full backyard. And because it's such a staple of Italian culture, it's always gone faster than I can dish out the next plate. The important thing is to wait until summer when tomatoes are juicy and ripe. Go for the really good ones, preferably from a farm stand—they are the star of the show here after all. But remember, don't worry about getting too fancy with it. Stick to the basics and keep the ingredients simple. It's a classic for a reason!

◆◆◆◆◆◆◆◆◆◆◆◆◆◆◆◆◆◆◆◆◆◆◆◆◆◆◆◆◆◆◆◆

2 large beefsteak tomatoes

1 lb [455 g] fresh mozzarella

2 sprigs fresh basil leaves

Kosher salt and freshly ground black pepper

Extra-virgin olive oil, for drizzling

Cut the tomatoes into ½ in [13 mm] thick slices and arrange on a serving platter. Cut the mozzarella into ½ in [13 mm] thick slices and shingle in with the tomatoes. Tuck the basil leaves in between each layer. Sprinkle a big pinch of salt and pepper over everything, then drizzle a good amount of olive oil over the top. Serve immediately.

Italian
GARDEN
SALAD

SERVES / 6 TO 8

5 or 6 large Jersey tomatoes
    or beefsteak tomatoes

1 English cucumber

1 green bell pepper

1 small red onion

1 long hot pepper (optional)

Large handful of fresh basil
    leaves

¼ cup [60 ml] extra-virgin
    olive oil

Kosher salt and freshly
    ground black pepper

◆◆◆◆◆◆◆◆◆◆◆◆◆◆◆◆◆◆◆◆◆◆◆◆

I feel like I was born eating this salad. My entire life, this was always on the table when vegetables were fresh and ripe. It's one of those things that I start to miss when I haven't had it lately, but I do my best to wait until summer, when my garden is getting full and my tomatoes and cucumbers are ready to be picked. There's nothing like a fresh salad with perfectly ripe produce.

◆◆◆◆◆◆◆◆◆◆◆◆◆◆◆◆◆◆◆◆◆◆

Cut the tomatoes into wedges and transfer to a large bowl. Cut the cucumber into ½ in [13 mm] thick slices and add to the bowl. Cut the bell pepper into strips. Halve and thinly slice the red onion. Thinly slice the long hot (if using). Everything goes in the bowl, along with the basil. I like to keep the leaves whole, but you can chop them if you want.

Season with the olive oil and several big pinches of salt and pepper. I like to let everything sit for at least 30 minutes before serving. The vegetables will start releasing their own juices and intensifying in flavor.

SOUR CREAM

Potato Salad

SERVES / 6

1¾ lb [795 g] baby Yukon gold potatoes (or one 28 oz [795 g] bag)

1 cup [240 g] sour cream

1 cup [240 g] mayonnaise

1 celery stalk, diced

1 large shallot, diced

2 Tbsp finely chopped fresh dill

2 Tbsp Potato Salad Seasoning (page 32)

◆◆◆◆◆◆◆◆◆◆◆◆◆◆◆◆◆◆◆◆◆◆◆◆◆◆◆◆◆◆◆

When my family goes to the shore in the summer, they can count on this potato salad showing up a few times a week. I used to make an Italian version—tossed in a vinaigrette with green beans and olives—until one year our friend from Texas, TJ, was visiting us down the shore. He was telling me about the way his mom always made potato salad, a bowl of creamy, stick-to-your-ribs goodness, and it sounded great. So I said, "Call her up!" We called his mom back in Texas, she dictated the recipe to me, I changed a few things around based on what I had in the house, and it became one of my greatest hits. When I make this, I have to make mountains of it because everyone wants to take some home.

◆◆◆◆◆◆◆◆◆◆◆◆◆◆◆◆◆◆◆◆◆◆◆◆◆◆◆◆◆

In a large pot, combine the potatoes and enough cold salted water to cover. Set over medium heat and bring to a simmer. Cook until the potatoes can be easily pierced with a fork, 15 to 20 minutes. Drain the potatoes.

In a large bowl, whisk together the sour cream, mayonnaise, celery, shallot, dill, and potato salad seasoning. Add the potatoes and lightly mash a few for added texture. Fold everything together until the potatoes are coated. Serve hot or cover the bowl with plastic wrap and refrigerate for 2 hours, until chilled, or overnight.

MAKE YOUR Apron FABULOUS

Let's have a little chat about a kitchen essential that often gets overlooked: the humble apron. As the one who's doing all the cooking, you're never dressed in your best and ready to go. You're doing all the heavy lifting, making sure your guests are walking into a memorable dining experience, and you gave up on the myth that you'll have time to slip away and get ready hours ago. So while they're looking perfect in their makeup and jewelry, you look like a hot mess. Well, I have a simple solution for you: Make your apron fabulous!

In the hustle and bustle of the kitchen, the apron stands as your faithful companion, protecting your clothes from the inevitable splatters and spills. But it's time to recognize the apron's true potential and choose one that reflects your personality and style. Treat it as an extension of your wardrobe, your personal fashion statement while you work your magic in the kitchen. When you look good, you feel good, and that confidence radiates. Tying on a fabulous apron elevates your mood and mindset, reminding you that you're the real star of the show here. As the culinary queen, you should command your kitchen with style and grace. Think of your apron as a symbol of empowerment, a reminder of your strength and expertise. It's not just about the practicality; it's about owning your role and embracing the beauty of your craft.

Cooking is an art, and your apron is your canvas for creative expression. Whether it's a vibrant floral design, a sleek modern cut, a retro-inspired pattern, a funny quote, or your dream bikini bod, let your apron make a statement about who you are. I have a few different aprons with colors and patterns to fit my mood and inspire me in the kitchen. Embrace the opportunity to express your unique self in the kitchen, and let your apron become a signature piece that sets you apart. And the best part is there's zero risk that someone will be wearing the same thing!

So go ahead and make your apron fabulous. Step into the kitchen with style, exude confidence, and celebrate your individuality. Own your role as a culinary goddess and remember that you deserve to look and feel fabulous, even in the middle of kitchen chaos. Trust me, it's a game changer.

Grilled SALMON SALAD

SERVES / 4 TO 8

This is a simple, light summer salad. I use my same secret technique from the Smoky Grilled Peaches (page 95) and line the grill with foil so the salmon stays intact without breaking. Feel free to mix and match oils, vinegars, and salad ingredients, but this recipe is my preferred version. I like to serve it on a platter, big and rustic and family style to celebrate peak summer freshness.

4 salmon fillets, skin on

1/4 cup [60 ml] extra-virgin olive oil, plus more for brushing

Juice of 1 navel orange

Kosher salt and freshly ground black pepper

4 cups [80 g] baby spinach

2 green onions, white and green parts, thinly sliced

1 small red onion, thinly sliced

1 medium navel orange, peeled and cut (see Note)

3 Tbsp balsamic vinegar

1 garlic clove, minced

4 oz [115 g] goat cheese

1/2 cup [60 g] toasted walnuts, roughly chopped

Line the grill grates with aluminum foil. Prepare the grill for medium heat (about 350°F [180°C]).

Brush the salmon skin with olive oil. Brush the flesh with the orange juice. Season both sides generously with salt and pepper. Just before grilling, brush the foil with plenty of olive oil. This will make sure the salmon cooks perfectly without getting stuck.

Arrange the fillets on the grill and close the lid. Grill for 8 to 10 minutes, until the salmon is pale pink and easily flakes when tested with a fork. Remove from the grill to rest.

In a large bowl, toss the spinach, green onions, red onion, and orange segments. In a small bowl, whisk together the olive oil, balsamic vinegar, garlic, any reserved orange juice from the segments, and a good pinch of salt and pepper. Drizzle the dressing over the salad and toss to coat. Arrange on a large serving platter or divide among plates. Finish the salad with crumbles of goat cheese and a sprinkle of walnuts. Arrange the salmon fillets around the platter or on individual plates before serving.

NOTE

For perfect orange pieces, cut a small slice from the top and the bottom of the citrus so you have a clear view of the fruit inside. Set the citrus on one of the flat sides and run your knife from top to bottom, following the curve of the fruit. The goal is to remove the peel and white pith, but ideally not too much fruit. Rotate the fruit as you slice away small sections. Hold the fruit over a small bowl and carefully slide your knife in between the fruit and the white membrane to release the segments. Let the pieces drop into the bowl, then squeeze the leftover orange to release any extra juices into the bowl.

Easy BLT DIP

(SERVES / 8)

1 lb [455 g] bacon

1 cup [240 g] sour cream

1 cup [240 g] mayonnaise

1 cup [80 g] shredded Cheddar cheese

1 roma tomato, diced

1 green onion, white and green parts, minced

Potato chips (preferably Ruffles), for serving

This crowd-pleasing dip is perfect to have when hosting a hot summer night barbecue or the Super Bowl. It uses lots of ingredients I usually have on hand, so it's easy to make on demand. It's also my secret weapon to guarantee that everyone is glued to the bowl and out of my kitchen. I usually serve it with chips, but it's great with pretzels, Crostini (page 154), cubes of pumpernickel, torn Italian bread, or just a spoon.

Preheat the oven to 450°F [230°C]. Line two rimmed baking sheets with aluminum foil.

Arrange the bacon pieces slightly spaced out on the two baking sheets. Bake for 10 to 15 minutes, rotating the sheet halfway through, until the bacon is crispy. Remove to paper towels to cool, then crumble the bacon.

In a medium bowl, stir together the sour cream, mayonnaise, Cheddar, tomato, green onion, and half of the bacon. Cover with plastic wrap and refrigerate for at least 2 hours, until chilled, or overnight. Top with the remaining bacon and serve with plenty of chips for dipping.

Juicy TURKEY BURGERS

SERVES / 6

Honestly, sometimes I need a break from beef. My daughter, Lauren, doesn't digest beef well, so I started playing around with a juicy, flavorful turkey burger and struck gold. They're a staple for when I'm cooking indoors or out, and somehow always seem to go as fast as the beef burgers.

3 slices white sandwich bread, roughly torn

1 egg

3 Tbsp mayonnaise

½ small red onion, roughly chopped

½ small yellow onion, roughly chopped

2 Tbsp fresh dill leaves

¼ tsp mustard powder

1 lb [455 g] ground turkey

Kosher salt and freshly ground black pepper

6 toasted buns, for serving

In a food processor, combine the torn bread, egg, mayonnaise, red onion, yellow onion, dill, and mustard powder. Pulse about six times until everything is finely chopped and combined. Scrape the mixture into a large bowl. Add the turkey and a couple generous pinches of salt and pepper. Use your hands to mix until combined, being careful not to overwork the meat.

Line a rimmed baking sheet with parchment paper. Separate the mixture into six portions and form into patties, evenly spaced on the baking sheet. Freeze the burgers for 15 minutes to firm up before grilling.

Meanwhile, prepare one half of the grill for high heat (about 450°F [230°C]) and leave the other half unlit. When the burgers are firm, lay them on the high heat side of the grill and close the lid. Grill for 3 minutes, then flip. Close the lid and grill for 3 more minutes. Move the burgers to the unlit side of the grill and close the lid. Let them continue to cook in the ambient heat for about 4 minutes, until the burgers are cooked through or register at least 165°F [74°C] on a meat thermometer. Serve on toasted buns with your favorite condiments.

 These burgers can also be made on the stove. Heat 2 Tbsp of olive oil in a large skillet over medium heat. When the oil shimmers, work in batches to sear the burgers for 5 minutes on each side until nicely browned and cooked through.

Grilled
CHICKEN
WINGS

WITH BALSAMIC BARBECUE SAUCE

SERVES / **4 TO 6**

When the grill is going, the men in my family start sniffing around for one thing: chicken wings. I don't blame them; it's hard to resist a great wing. I like to make them with this punchy barbecue sauce that's sweet, sticky, and finger-licking good. When I know it's going to be a day of big eating, I just double or triple this recipe and keep the wings coming all afternoon. A big pile of these will feed a crowd and leave everyone satisfied.

3 lb [1.4 kg] chicken wings, flats and drumettes separated

2 Tbsp vegetable oil

Kosher salt and freshly ground black pepper

1½ cups [360 ml] Balsamic Barbecue Sauce (recipe follows)

In a large bowl, toss the wings with the vegetable oil and a couple good pinches of salt and pepper until the wings are coated.

Prepare the grill for medium heat (about 350°F [180°C]). Grill the wings for 10 to 12 minutes, flipping halfway, until charred and cooked through.

In a clean large bowl, toss the grilled wings with 1 cup [240 ml] of the balsamic barbecue sauce. Return the wings to the grill and cook for 4 minutes, flipping halfway, until the sauce is nice and sticky. Return the wings to the bowl and toss with the remaining ½ cup [120 ml] of sauce. Stack the wings on a platter and serve immediately.

RECIPE CONTINUES

BALSAMIC BARBECUE SAUCE

MAKES 1½ CUPS [360 ML]

2 Tbsp extra-virgin olive oil

1 white onion, finely diced

2 garlic cloves, minced

1 cup [240 ml] balsamic vinegar

2 Tbsp dark brown sugar

½ tsp red pepper flakes

½ cup [170 g] ketchup

¼ cup [85 g] honey

2 Tbsp spicy brown mustard

2 Tbsp Worcestershire sauce

1 Tbsp smoked paprika

1 Tbsp liquid smoke (optional)

Kosher salt and freshly ground black pepper

In a small saucepan over medium heat, heat the olive oil. When the oil shimmers, add the onion and garlic. Sauté until the onion is translucent, about 5 minutes. Stir in the balsamic, brown sugar, and red pepper flakes. Simmer until the mixture is reduced by half, about 10 minutes. Add the ketchup, honey, mustard, Worcestershire sauce, paprika, liquid smoke (if using), and a big pinch of salt and pepper. When the mixture comes to a boil, turn the heat to low and simmer for about 15 minutes, until glossy and thick. Use an immersion blender, or transfer the sauce to a regular blender, and blend until smooth. Transfer to an airtight container and refrigerate until ready to use, or up to 4 weeks.

NOTE: The balsamic barbecue sauce doesn't have to stick to just wings. Make a big batch and slather it over everything you're grilling, all summer.

SHORT RIB *Sliders*

SERVES / 6

---

3 lb [1.4 kg] bone-in short ribs

Kosher salt and freshly ground black pepper

2 Tbsp extra-virgin olive oil

1 medium white onion, halved and thinly sliced

1 cup [240 ml] chicken stock

One 14.5 oz [410 g] can crushed tomatoes

½ cup [100 g] dark brown sugar

12 to 18 toasted slider buns, prepared coleslaw, and sliced pickles, for serving

---

These sliders are so stupidly delicious: After a slow simmer in fragrant onions, tomatoes, and brown sugar, the short ribs are so tender they melt in your mouth. I like to make a big batch of the meat and let it sit for a day or two to let all the flavors soak in and really develop. When I went on Kelly Ripa's show, I made these for her and Michael Strahan, and the entire crew went nuts for them. So make more than you think you need! Trust me, they'll disappear as fast as you can make them.

Preheat the oven to 250°F [120°C].

Season the ribs all over with generous pinches of salt and pepper. In a Dutch oven over high heat, heat the olive oil. When the oil shimmers, arrange the short ribs in an even layer. Sear for about 5 minutes on each side, until nicely browned. Turn the heat to low and add the onion, chicken stock, tomatoes, and brown sugar. Bring the mixture to a simmer, cover, and slide the pot into the oven. Braise for about 2 hours, until the meat is barely on the bone.

Use tongs to remove the bones and transfer the meat to a large plate. Return the sauce to medium heat and simmer until glossy and thick, about 5 minutes. Add the meat and any collected juices back into the sauce and stir to combine.

Pile the meat onto toasted slider buns (this makes between 12 and 18 sliders, depending how generously you portion the meat). Finish with a little coleslaw and a pickle slice before pressing the top on and serving.

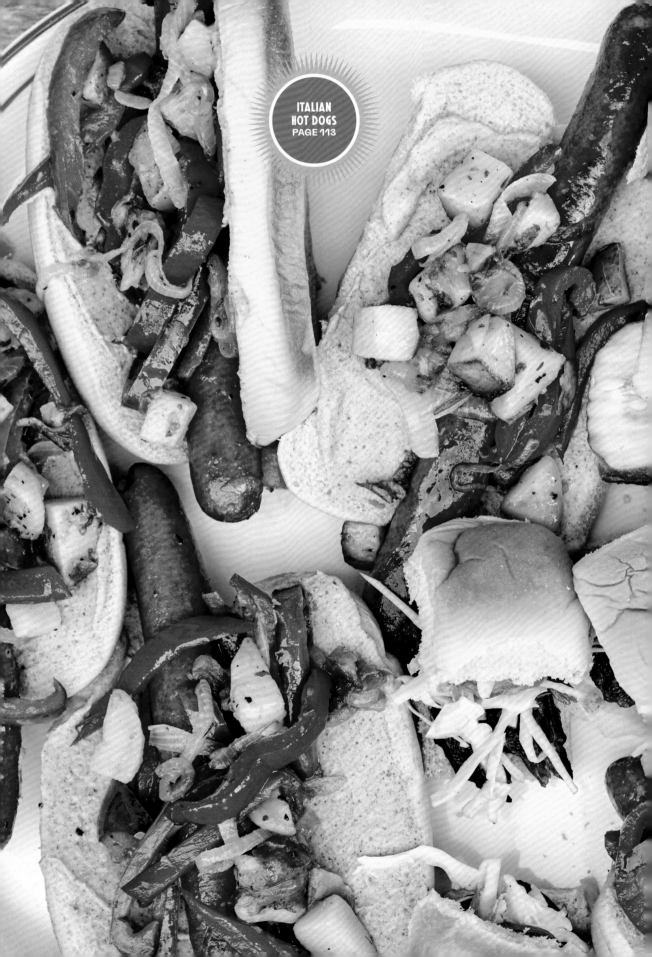

ITALIAN
HOT DOGS
PAGE 113

SHORT RIB
SLIDERS
PAGE 109

ITALIAN *Hot Dogs*

SERVES / 6

6 baby red potatoes

2 Tbsp extra-virgin olive oil

1 green bell pepper,
cut into strips

1 red bell pepper,
cut into strips

1 white onion, halved and
sliced

1/2 tsp dried oregano

Kosher salt and freshly
ground black pepper

6 hot dogs

6 toasted hot dog buns and
spicy brown mustard, for
serving

Al and I used to go to a spot in Newark, just a guy with a street corner hot dog cart, to get these. They were so good that I started making them for us at home whenever we got a craving. Inspired by the classic Italian sausage and pepper sandwich, they're messy, oily, robust, colorful, delicious, filling, and bursting with flavor. Can you tell how much I love them?

In a medium saucepan, combine the potatoes and enough cold salted water to cover. Set over medium heat and bring to a simmer. Cook until the potatoes can be easily pierced with a fork, 10 to 15 minutes. Drain the potatoes and rinse under cold water. Cut the potatoes into cubes.

In a large skillet over medium heat, heat the olive oil. When the oil shimmers, add the peppers, onion, and potatoes. Sauté until the peppers and onion are soft, about 5 minutes. Stir in the oregano and a good pinch of salt and pepper. Push the veggies to one side and lay the hot dogs in the skillet. Sear for about 4 minutes on each side until warmed through, letting the veggies char slightly.

Split the hot dog buns and spread a little mustard on both sides. Use tongs to set a hot dog in the center, then top with the veggie mixture. Serve hot.

 These dogs can also be made on the grill. After the potatoes are cooked, prepare the grill for medium heat (about 350°F [180°C]). Set an oven-safe skillet on one side of the grill and follow the directions for cooking the vegetables. The hot dogs can either sear in the skillet or go directly on the grill to char.

One-Pan BRANZINO & TOMATOES

(SERVES / 4)

This dish screams summertime: It's simple, it's fresh, and it has a lot of vibrant flavors. I hate standing over a sweltering stove in the summer as much as the next person, but the lucky thing about this is if you take the time to prep all your ingredients first, you won't have to be near a flame for more than 15 minutes, I promise. I love cooking with wine, but I also think liqueurs can add a nice little surprise to a dish like this. The sweet citrus flavor of limoncello is a perfect partner for the fish.

½ cup [70 g] seasoned bread crumbs

4 skin-on branzino fillets, bones removed

Kosher salt and freshly ground black pepper

2 Tbsp extra-virgin olive oil

6 Roma tomatoes, diced

1 Tbsp fresh thyme leaves

1 Tbsp fresh oregano leaves

2 Tbsp dry white wine

2 Tbsp limoncello liqueur

2 Tbsp unsalted butter

In a large nonstick skillet, spread the bread crumbs evenly. Set over medium heat and toast, stirring often, until golden brown, about 4 minutes. Remove to a bowl and wipe the skillet clean.

Pat the branzino dry with paper towels and season well with a good pinch of salt and pepper on both sides. In the same large skillet over medium-high heat, heat the oil. When the oil shimmers, lay the fillets, skin-side down, in the skillet. Use a spatula to press on each fillet to make sure the skin is fully touching the skillet. Sear for 3 minutes, then flip. Continue to cook for 30 to 60 seconds, until the flesh is fully opaque. Transfer the fillets to a serving platter, skin-side up.

Set the same skillet back over medium heat. Add the tomatoes, thyme, and oregano. Cook until the tomatoes are vibrant and the herbs are fragrant, about 1 minute. Add the wine, limoncello, and a good pinch of salt and pepper. Let the mixture simmer until the liquid is reduced by half, about 2 minutes. Add the butter and swirl the skillet as it melts to incorporate. When the sauce is glossy, remove from the heat.

Spoon the sauce over the branzino fillets. Finish with a sprinkle of bread crumbs before serving.

Linguine
WITH
CLAMS

SERVES / **4 to 6**

This is another classic shore dish. Every year, we have lobster night, where Al and the boys buy a boatload of shellfish. I make a mega-size version of this recipe, no less than 5 lb [2.3 kg] of linguine, and it all goes. It feels like the second I pour everything onto the clams, the entire house magically appears, forks out, trying to grab some. For me, this is what summer is all about.

- ¼ cup [60 ml] extra-virgin olive oil, plus more for serving
- 4 garlic cloves, minced
- ½ tsp red pepper flakes
- ½ cup [120 ml] dry white wine
- ½ cup [120 ml] chicken stock or seafood stock
- 1 lb [455 g] littleneck clams, scrubbed
- 1 lb [455 g] dried linguine
- 3 Tbsp finely chopped fresh parsley
- Juice of 1 lemon
- Kosher salt and freshly ground black pepper
- Grated pecorino cheese, for serving

In a Dutch oven over medium heat, heat the oil. When the oil shimmers, add the garlic and red pepper flakes. Sauté until lightly browned, about 1 minute. Add the white wine and chicken stock. Simmer until the liquid is reduced by half, about 6 minutes. Add the clams and cover. Let the clams steam until fully opened, about 10 minutes.

Meanwhile, bring a large pot of salted water to a boil over high heat. Cook the linguine to al dente according to the package directions. Reserve ½ cup [120 ml] of the pasta water, then drain the pasta.

Add the pasta and ¼ cup [60 ml] of the reserved pasta water to the clams. Simmer, tossing constantly to coat the pasta in the sauce, until the sauce is nicely thick, about 2 minutes. Add the parsley, lemon juice, and plenty of black pepper and toss. Add a splash more of the remaining pasta water as needed. Season with salt.

Transfer the pasta to a large serving plate. Drizzle with some more olive oil and garnish with a few sprinkles of pecorino before serving.

N·O·T·E

Don't microwave leftover pasta! Add it to a skillet with a splash of water, set over medium heat, and toss until warmed through.

Molto Buono

◆◆◆◆◆◆◆◆◆◆

This is the food I love the most.
These recipes transport me back to
generations of Sunday suppers around a crowded
table, laughter echoing through the air, and
love infused in every bite. They're the memories
that make my heart sing and bring a smile
to my face. Molto buono!

Burrata WITH PROSCIUTTO & RED PEPPERS

SERVES / 2 TO 4

These are flavors that run through an Italian's veins. There's just nothing like the combination of roasted red peppers, prosciutto, cheese, basil, and balsamic. This dish is a Sunday staple in my house. I don't know why, but for me, mozzarella is for every day and Burrata is for Sunday. It feels special, like an event, and I spend all week looking forward to it.

4 Roasted Red Peppers (page 39)

4 oz [115 g] thinly sliced prosciutto

8 oz [230 g] fresh Burrata cheese

2 sprigs fresh basil leaves

Extra-virgin olive oil

Balsamic vinegar

Freshly ground black pepper

Layer the red peppers, prosciutto, Burrata, and basil on a serving plate. Drizzle with a good amount of olive oil and balsamic vinegar, finish with plenty of black pepper, and serve.

Giambotta

2 Tbsp extra-virgin olive oil

1 large white onion, diced

4 garlic cloves, crushed or minced

2 zucchini, cubed

2 medium russet potatoes, diced

2 green bell peppers, diced

Kosher salt and freshly ground black pepper

8 oz [230 g] green beans, trimmed and cut into 1 in [2.5 cm] pieces

One 28 oz [795 g] can whole peeled tomatoes

Pecorino rind (optional)

½ cup [120 ml] dry white wine

2 cups [480 ml] vegetable broth

2 sprigs fresh parsley leaves

1 sprig fresh oregano leaves

Red pepper flakes

One 15.5 oz [440 g] can cannellini beans, rinsed and drained

One 16 oz [455 g] bag frozen peas

Pecorino cheese and crusty bread, for serving

The best thing about giambotta is there are no wrong answers. It's about as traditional as Italian country cooking gets, an easy soupy stew to celebrate the summer vegetable harvest. I like to stick to the classics and use zucchini, peppers, and potatoes. But every family has their own way of doing things, so grab whatever you have. Simmering in tomatoes, wine, and broth saturates the veggies with tons of flavor, and a few sprigs of fresh herbs and a pecorino rind are all the seasoning you need. (Plus a shake or two of some red pepper flakes to spice it up, if you choose!)

In a large saucepan over medium heat, heat the olive oil. When the oil shimmers, add the onion and garlic. Sauté until the onion is translucent, about 5 minutes.

Add the zucchini, potatoes, and peppers, along with a good pinch of salt and pepper. Sauté, stirring often, until the peppers and zucchini start to soften, about 5 minutes. Add the green beans and can of tomatoes. (If you have a rind of pecorino, throw in a 1 in [2.5 cm] chunk!) Stir in the white wine, broth, parsley, oregano, and a pinch of red pepper flakes. Bring to a simmer, then cover and turn the heat to medium-low. Simmer until the potatoes can be easily pierced with a fork, 25 to 30 minutes.

Stir in the cannellini beans and peas. Taste for seasoning. Simmer, uncovered, for about 10 minutes more, until the beans and peas are warmed through. Remove and discard the rind (if using). Serve immediately with pecorino for grating and plenty of bread for dipping.

Pasta
E PISELLI
{PASTA & PEAS}

SERVES / **6 TO 8**

2 Tbsp extra-virgin olive oil

1 large white onion, diced

5 garlic cloves, smashed

4 Roma tomatoes, diced

Two 14.5 oz [410 g] cans chicken stock

Kosher salt and freshly ground black pepper

Pecorino rind (optional)

1 lb [455 g] dried small shells or tubetti pasta

One 16 oz [455 g] bag frozen peas

Pecorino cheese, for serving

◆◆◆◆◆◆◆◆◆◆◆◆◆◆◆◆◆◆◆◆◆◆◆◆

This simple pasta is without a doubt one of my very favorites. My grandma and parents would make this all the time, an easy way to feed eleven hungry kids. So there's a lot of nostalgia for me; it's one of those dishes that just tastes like home. When we were short on a full 1 lb [455 g] of pasta, my grandma would gather up a bunch of different pasta shapes, whatever bits of boxes were lying around. She would break them up with a meat tenderizer and throw them into the pot, so we would get all different textures and shapes in every bite.

◆◆◆◆◆◆◆◆◆◆◆◆◆◆◆◆◆◆◆◆◆◆◆◆

In a Dutch oven over medium heat, heat the olive oil. When the oil shimmers, add the onion and garlic. Sauté until the onion is translucent, about 5 minutes. Stir in the tomatoes and simmer until softened, about 4 minutes. Add the stock and a big pinch of salt and pepper. (If you have a rind of pecorino, throw in a 1 in [2.5 cm] chunk!) Bring to a boil, then turn the heat to low and simmer until the flavors meld, about 15 minutes.

Meanwhile, bring a large pot of salted water to a boil over high heat. Cook the shells to al dente according to the package directions. Drain the pasta.

Stir the pasta and frozen peas into the sauce until completely coated. Continue to simmer, stirring often, until the peas are vibrant green, about 2 minutes. Remove and discard the rind (if using).

Ladle into bowls and serve with plenty of pecorino grated on top.

Don't microwave leftover pasta! Add it to a skillet with a splash of water, set over medium heat, and toss until warmed through.

THE WHOLE GARDEN Pasta Primavera

- ¼ cup [60 ml] extra-virgin olive oil
- 4 oz [115 g] baby bella mushrooms, sliced
- 2 medium carrots, julienned
- 1 zucchini, julienned
- 1 green bell pepper, cut into strips
- 1 medium onion, halved and sliced
- 3 garlic cloves, minced
- 6 plum tomatoes, diced
- 2 cups [240 g] frozen peas
- Kosher salt
- 1 cup [240 ml] vegetable broth
- Pecorino rind (optional)
- 1 lb [455 g] dried spaghetti or angel hair
- 2 Tbsp finely chopped fresh parsley
- 2 Tbsp finely chopped fresh basil

This pasta is like sunshine in a bowl. Just thinking about it makes me feel light and good and happy. I like to use whatever fresh ingredients I can find, which means I'm constantly changing the lineup here. Use this recipe as a starting point, but don't feel like you have to follow it exactly. It's great in the summer, but I especially like it in the winter when I need some extra warm comfort.

In a Dutch oven over medium heat, heat the olive oil. When the oil shimmers, add the mushrooms, carrots, zucchini, bell pepper, onion, and garlic. Sauté, stirring often, until the vegetables are tender, about 5 minutes. Stir in the tomatoes, peas, and a couple big pinches of salt. Stir in the broth. (If you have a rind of pecorino, throw in a 1 in [2.5 cm] chunk!) Bring to a simmer, then remove from the heat to let the flavors meld.

Meanwhile, bring a large pot of salted water to a boil over high heat. Cook the spaghetti to al dente according to the package directions. Drain the pasta.

Add the pasta to the vegetables and return to medium heat. Simmer, tossing constantly to coat the pasta in the sauce, until everything is combined and the sauce is slightly thickened, about 2 minutes. Remove and discard the rind (if using). Remove from the heat and stir in the parsley and basil before serving.

Don't microwave leftover pasta! Add it to a skillet with a splash of water, set over medium heat, and toss until warmed through.

Eggplant PARMIGIANA

This is Al's absolute favorite thing. I usually make this for him as a treat on Father's Day, and even after all these years, his eyes still light up. I like to keep my eggplant thin so it gets soft and almost melting while it bakes. Plus there's the oily, crispy coating, thick marinara, and layers of cheese. OK, I understand why he loves it so much! This usually doesn't stick around long in my house, but if I have any leftovers, I love to eat it the next day as a sandwich, stuffed in a hero or between two slices of white bread.

4 eggplants (about 4 lb [1.8 kg]), peeled and cut into ¼ in [6 mm] thick rounds

Kosher salt and freshly ground black pepper

4 eggs

4 cups [560 g] seasoned bread crumbs

2 cups [480 ml] vegetable oil, plus more as needed

One 24 oz [680 g] jar marinara, plus 2 cups [480 g] marinara or leftover Sunday Gravy (page 144)

8 Tbsp [15 g] grated Parmesan cheese

2 cups [160 g] shredded low-moisture mozzarella cheese

Chopped fresh basil, for serving

Line two rimmed baking sheets with paper towels and spread out the eggplant rounds in an even layer. Heavily salt both sides of the rounds and leave to drain for 15 minutes.

Preheat the oven to 400°F [200°C]. Coat a 9 by 13 in [23 by 33 cm] baking pan with nonstick spray.

In a medium bowl, whisk the eggs with 2 Tbsp of water. In a separate medium bowl, spread out the bread crumbs. Pat the eggplant rounds dry with more paper towels. In a large skillet, start heating the vegetable oil over medium-low heat.

I like to designate a wet hand (usually my left hand) and a dry hand (usually my right hand). With your wet hand, dip an eggplant round into the eggs, then lift to let the excess drip off. Drop into the bread crumbs and use your dry hand to sprinkle bread crumbs to cover. Press and flip to make sure the round is fully covered, then transfer to a wire rack.

Test the oil by dipping in an edge of a coated eggplant round. If the oil bubbles nicely, it's ready to fry. Add enough rounds to fill the skillet without crowding it, usually three or four rounds. Fry for about 2 minutes per side until the coating is golden brown and crisp. Return the fried rounds to the wire rack to drain. Continue coating and frying all the rounds, filling a second wire rack if you need it.

Now it's time to assemble. Spread ½ cup [120 ml] of the marinara along the bottom of the prepared baking pan. Use about a fourth of the eggplant rounds to create an even layer, overlapping the rounds as needed. Sprinkle 2 Tbsp of the Parmesan and ½ cup [40 g] of the mozzarella over the rounds. Repeat the process to build four layers.

Bake for 20 to 25 minutes, until the cheese is melted and bubbly. Remove from the oven and rest for 15 minutes before sprinkling with basil, slicing, and serving.

FOUR CHEESE *Lasagna*

---

1 lb [455 g] dried lasagna
noodles

8 cups [1.9 L] marinara

2 lb [910 g] ricotta cheese

1 lb [455 g] mozzarella
cheese, (preferably
whole milk, low-moisture
mozzarella), grated

4 oz [115 g] Parmesan cheese,
grated

4 oz [115 g] pecorino cheese,
grated

I don't make lasagna that often, as I prefer whipping up other pasta dishes. But I roll this out when I need to feed a hungry army because it always hits the spot. When my full family all gathers at my house, it's what everyone expects to find on the table. The great thing about lasagna is it was practically designed to be made a day ahead. It reheats perfectly and the flavor only improves overnight. I make a couple at a time to make sure there's plenty to go around, plus a couple extra so everyone can leave with leftovers.

Preheat the oven to 350°F [180°C]. Coat a 9 by 13 in [23 by 33 cm] baking dish with nonstick spray.

Bring a large pot of salted water to a boil over high heat. Cook the lasagna noodles to al dente according to the package directions. Drain the pasta.

Spread 2 cups [480 ml] of the marinara along the bottom of the prepared baking dish, then arrange a layer of lasagna noodles. Dollop with one-fourth of the ricotta, then sprinkle one-fourth each of the mozzarella, Parmesan, and pecorino. Continue building in the same order to create four layers, ending with a cheese topping.

Bake for 40 to 45 minutes, until the cheese is browned and the lasagna is bubbling. Remove from the oven and let cool in the pan for 20 minutes to set. Cut into squares and serve.

NOTE

To make this even more
flavorful, I like to buy the
no-boil lasagna noodles
and soak them in chicken
broth for 10 minutes
before assembling.

Decorate YOUR HOUSE

When my kids were growing up, we loved decorating for every holiday. Valentine's Day meant paper hearts on the windows. Thanksgiving was hay and pumpkins outside. Christmas was a big event with a 20 ft [6 m] tree and a lot of micromanaging from me. (When it was all done, you would have thought you were walking into Neiman Marcus.) Now I have an empty nest, but it makes me so proud to see my kids carry on the decorating traditions in their own homes. Even though I've scaled back on my ambitions, I still like to mark the year with thoughtful touches. Here are some easy tips to make your house festive all year:

1 KEEP IT SIMPLE. Taking inspiration from nature, like a fall centerpiece on the table or a few fresh flowers for spring, can be very effective. Or some small touches like incorporating seasonal colors or patterns into your table settings can make all the difference. Let the season and the holiday be your guide!

2 GET EVERYONE INVOLVED. Many hands make light work. But more importantly, it's an opportunity for family moments you'll remember for years. When the kids were little, the time we spent decorating inspired some of my favorite conversations and some of the biggest bloopers we still laugh about today. It's time together to mark the different seasons of life, and that's an invaluable experience.

3 PICK A SPOT. Don't worry about tackling the entire house; focus on just one area. If you're like me and the table is the center of your home, make sure it sparkles for the season. Or maybe your front stoop, entryway, windowsill, or staircase is the perfect place to decorate. Narrowing down to one place makes the project feel fun and manageable, not stressful and daunting. Because who needs that?

4 LIGHT IT UP. For me, lighting has always been the best way to set the mood. Of course, Christmas is all about the lights, but my kids loved getting creative with spooky Halloween lighting too. Colorful lights on the Fourth of July keep the mood going long after the fireworks are done. And my Thanksgiving table isn't set without lots and lots of candles. It's a simple thing that really makes all the difference.

5 MAKE IT PERSONAL. Don't spend time comparing yourself with your friends and neighbors. Find what speaks to you and make it a reflection of your story and traditions. Family heirlooms, sentimental ornaments, and school crafts from the kids are great ways to complement store-bought decorations. Photographs and cards from loved ones are a meaningful way to celebrate. Instead of loading up on a lot of junk, find the things that inspire you, because decorating should always be about creating special memories to last all year.

Ultimate CHICKEN PARM

SERVES / 8

My husband, Al, loves Eggplant Parmigiana (page 128), but my son Albie absolutely lives for chicken parm. We always tease him because it feels like the only thing he orders at a restaurant and it's what he most often requests when he's home. I think his body is mostly chicken parm at this point. I'll use jarred marinara in a pinch, but I really love to make this on Monday or Tuesday when I have leftover gravy from Sunday.

8 boneless, skinless chicken cutlets (about 2 lb [910 g]), pounded thin

Kosher salt and freshly ground black pepper

4 eggs

2 cups [280 g] seasoned bread crumbs

1½ cups [45 g] grated Parmesan cheese

2 cups [480 ml] vegetable oil, plus more as needed

2 cups [480 ml] leftover Sunday Gravy (page 144) or marinara, plus more warmed for serving

2 cups [160 g] shredded low-moisture mozzarella

2 Tbsp finely chopped fresh parsley

Set the broiler to high. Line a rimmed baking sheet with aluminum foil and set a wire rack on top.

Pat the chicken cutlets dry with paper towels and season generously with big pinches of salt and pepper. In a pie plate or cake pan, whisk the eggs. In another pie plate, stir together the bread crumbs and ½ cup [15 g] of the Parmesan. In a large skillet, start heating the vegetable oil over medium-low heat.

I like to designate a wet hand (usually my left hand) and a dry hand (usually my right hand). Working in batches of two cutlets, use your wet hand to dip the chicken into the eggs, then lift to let the excess drip off. Drop into the bread crumbs and use your dry hand to sprinkle bread crumbs to cover. Press and flip to make sure the cutlet is fully covered.

Test the oil by dipping in an edge of the coated cutlet. If the oil bubbles nicely, it's ready to fry. Add the two cutlets to the skillet and fry for about 2 minutes per side until the coating is golden brown and crisp. Transfer to the wire rack to drain. Continue coating and frying all the cutlets, filling the wire rack.

Now it's time to assemble. Spread ¼ cup [60 ml] of the gravy over each cutlet. Sprinkle 2 Tbsp of the Parmesan and ¼ cup [20 g] of the mozzarella over the sauce. Repeat the process on all the cutlets. Slide the entire baking sheet into the oven to broil for about 4 minutes, until the cheese is melted and starting to brown. Garnish with parsley and serve immediately with warm gravy on the side.

VEAL Saltimbocca

SERVES / 4 TO 8

This is a ready-in-a-flash, one-pan meal that I can make anytime anywhere and everyone's happy. Basically, it's a lifesaver. There aren't a lot of ingredients here, but somehow it's still loaded with tons of flavor. Sometimes I like to add fresh spinach to the pan to wilt or a couple handfuls of vegetables to bulk it up a little. But really, it's perfect on its own. If veal cutlets are too hard to find, go ahead and swap in chicken.

1 cup [140 g] all-purpose flour

8 veal cutlets (about 1 lb [455 g])

Kosher salt and freshly ground black pepper

16 pieces thinly sliced prosciutto

8 fresh sage leaves

¼ cup [60 ml] extra-virgin olive oil

¼ cup [60 ml] dry white wine

1 shallot, diced

1 cup [240 ml] chicken stock

4 Tbsp [55 g] unsalted butter

In a pie plate or cake pan, shake the flour into an even layer.

Working one at a time, pat a veal cutlet dry with paper towels. Place the cutlet between two pieces of plastic wrap and pound to about ⅛ in [3 mm] thick. Season lightly with salt and generously with pepper on both sides. Layer two pieces of prosciutto on one side of the veal, pressing to make sure it sticks. Lay a sage leaf in the middle of the prosciutto and use a toothpick to pin it on. Dredge the cutlet in the flour and shake off the excess. Set the cutlet on a wire rack and repeat with the remaining cutlets.

In a large skillet over medium heat, heat the olive oil. When the oil shimmers, use tongs to lower in two cutlets. Sear until the prosciutto is crisp and the veal is browned, about 2 minutes per side. Return to the wire rack and continue searing in batches.

Pour out the fat from the skillet and return to medium heat. Add the wine and shallot. Use a wooden spoon to scrape up any browned bits while the wine reduces by half, about 1 minute. Add the stock and a pinch of salt and pepper. Continue to simmer until the liquid reduces by half, about 3 minutes. Add the butter and swirl the pan as it melts. Use tongs to lower in half of the cutlets. Swirl the skillet to coat in the sauce, then transfer the cutlets to a serving plate. Repeat with the other half of the cutlets. Spoon the sauce over the plate and discard the toothpicks before serving.

POLLO al Mattone

{CHICKEN UNDER A BRICK}

SERVES / 4

One 3 to 4 lb [1.4 to 1.8 kg] chicken

1 Tbsp finely chopped fresh rosemary

1 Tbsp fresh thyme leaves

4 garlic cloves, minced

2 tsp kosher salt

2 tsp freshly ground black pepper

2 Tbsp vegetable oil

I love the slow process of roasting a chicken (see page 80 for more on that), but some nights I need to speed things up a little. We have the Tuscans to thank for this method of weighting the chicken down so the skin gets perfectly browned and the meat stays juicy and tender. It takes a little prep work to get the chicken ready, and I really recommend letting the seasoning seep into the chicken for as long as possible. But once you're cooking, the entire chicken is roasted in under 30 minutes.

NOTE To weigh down the chicken, I like to wrap the bottom of my Dutch oven in aluminum foil and set the whole thing on top. You could also wrap the bottom of a heavy cast-iron skillet. If you're going to use a regular skillet, wrap the bottom with foil, then wrap a brick or two heavy rocks in foil and set them inside the skillet to add extra weight.

Use kitchen scissors to cut the backbone out of the chicken. (The backbone is opposite the breast meat. You can also ask a butcher to do this for you.) Lay the chicken flat, cut-side down. Use both hands, like you're giving the chicken CPR, to press on the center of the breast and snap the bone. Pat the chicken dry on both sides with paper towels.

In a small bowl, mix the rosemary, thyme, garlic, salt, and pepper. Sprinkle the mixture evenly over the inside of the chicken, rub some under the skin, and sprinkle the rest on top of the skin. Set a wire rack in a rimmed baking sheet and place the chicken on top. Let rest at room temperature for 1 hour or, ideally, refrigerate the chicken (uncovered) overnight. Let the refrigerated chicken rest at room temperature for 30 minutes before cooking.

Preheat the oven to 500°F [260°C]. Set a large cast-iron or oven-safe skillet over high heat to preheat. Get your exhaust fan going and maybe open a window—you're going to need it!

When the oven is ready, add the vegetable oil to the skillet and swirl to make sure it coats the surface. Lay the chicken, skin-side down, in the skillet, then set your weight on top (see Note). Sear the chicken for about 15 minutes, until the skin is crisp and golden brown. Remove the weight and use two pairs of tongs to carefully flip the chicken skin-side up. Slide the skillet into the oven and continue to roast for 10 to 15 minutes until the breast reaches at least 160°F [71°C] and the thigh reaches at least 170°F [77°C] on a meat thermometer.

Use the double tongs again to transfer the chicken to a serving plate and let rest for 10 minutes before serving whole or carving.

SLOW-BRAISED *Braciole*

SERVES / 4

This was something I grew up eating, and probably every Italian remembers it from childhood. Everyone in my family made this—my grandparents, my parents, my aunts and uncles. I usually make it to add to my Sunday Gravy (page 144), but I love braciole on its own. When it melts in your mouth and is packed with flavor, it's unreal. It could be my entire meal. No bread, no nothing; just give me braciole!

1½ lb [680 g] flank steak or braciole slices

Kosher salt and freshly ground black pepper

¼ cup [10 g] finely chopped fresh parsley

¼ cup [8 g] grated Parmesan cheese

2 Tbsp grated pecorino cheese

4 garlic cloves, minced

2 Tbsp extra-virgin olive oil

½ cup [120 ml] dry white wine

One 14.5 oz [410 g] can crushed tomatoes

1 cup [240 ml] chicken or beef stock

Warm marinara sauce, for serving

Preheat the oven to 325°F [165°C].

Lay out the steak and pound any thicker areas for a relatively even piece. (If using braciole slices, shingle them to make one large surface.) Season generously with pinches of salt and pepper, then layer the parsley, Parmesan, pecorino, and garlic evenly over the top. Roll the steak into a long log and secure with string or toothpicks.

In a braiser or Dutch oven over high heat, heat the olive oil. When the oil shimmers, lower in the braciole. Sear on all sides until nicely browned, about 12 minutes total. Remove the braciole to a plate to rest.

Turn the heat to medium and add the wine. Use a wooden spoon to scrape up any browned bits from the bottom of the pot. When the wine has mostly evaporated, add the tomatoes, stock, and a good pinch of salt and pepper. Stir until the sauce comes to a simmer, then nestle the braciole in the sauce and cover.

Transfer the pot to the oven and braise for 1 hour. Remove the lid and flip the braciole. Continue to braise, uncovered, for 30 minutes, until the meat is nicely browned and very tender. Discard the braising liquid and the string or toothpicks and move the meat to a cutting board. Slice thin and serve with marinara over the top.

Manzo MEATBALLS

SERVES / 6

- 8 garlic cloves
- 7 slices white sandwich bread
- 8 oz [230 g] ground beef
- 8 oz [230 g] ground pork
- 8 oz [230 g] ground veal (see Note)
- 1 egg
- 3 cups [720 ml] whole milk
- ½ cup [30 g] grated pecorino cheese
- Kosher salt and freshly ground black pepper
- ¼ cup [60 ml] vegetable oil

Al says he married me for my meatballs. If they were good then, they're even better now! They're the consummate Caroline Manzo dish, what I'm known for and what people request when they come over. Usually my family will call before Sunday dinner, wanting to know what's on the menu. If the meatballs aren't on the list, they say they're not coming just to pressure me to make them. Even my granddaughter bullies me for them. These are made with a mixture of beef, pork, and veal, for tons of flavor. There's an obscene amount of milk in these, to the point that it'll feel like you're doing it wrong. Trust the process and you'll have meatballs that are crispy on the outside and creamy, almost custardy, on the inside. I sometimes throw them in my Sunday Gravy (page 144) or toss them in some marinara. But with my family hovering around, they never make it to the sauce. Sometimes they make it to the Antipasti Spread (page 153), but usually the vultures are standing around picking them right out of the pan.

In a food processor, pulse the garlic cloves about four times to roughly chop. Working in batches as needed, tear the slices of bread into the food processor and pulse about six times to make rough bread crumbs. Scrape the mixture into a large bowl. Add the beef, pork, veal, egg, milk, pecorino, and a big pinch of salt and pepper. Use your hands to mix until combined, being careful not to overwork the meat. It's going to be very loose, almost runny, but just holding together.

In a large skillet over medium heat, heat the vegetable oil. When the oil shimmers, use two soup spoons to scoop and scrape the meatballs into the oil. Continue scooping until the skillet is full, but not crowded. Fry until browned all over, flipping halfway, about 6 minutes total. Remove to paper towels to drain while scooping and frying the next batch.

N·O·T·E

Substitute extra beef or pork if ground veal is hard to find.

MANZO
MEATBALLS
PAGE 139

Turkey MEATBALLS

MAKES / **ABOUT 24 MEATBALLS**

8 baby bella mushrooms, roughly chopped

2 cups [40 g] baby spinach

1 zucchini, roughly chopped

1 white onion, roughly chopped

4 garlic cloves

1 lb [455 g] ground turkey

1 cup [140 g] seasoned bread crumbs

1 egg

2 Tbsp mayonnaise

Kosher salt and freshly ground black pepper

These meatballs are my daughter Lauren's favorite. She has some dietary issues where beef and pork are tough for her, so these are her special plate of Sunday meatballs. But they've started catching on, and it feels like I have to make bigger and bigger batches every Sunday. In the grand tradition of kids everywhere, my granddaughter, Markie, doesn't like anything green or remotely healthy. But even she will devour these sneaky vegetable-filled versions in a flash. Even beyond Sunday, I make them just to have around for eggs, sandwiches, or a random craving.

Set racks in the upper and lower thirds of the oven. Preheat the oven to 400°F [200°C]. Line two rimmed baking sheets with parchment paper.

In a food processor, combine the mushrooms, spinach, zucchini, onion, and garlic. Pulse about six times until all the vegetables are finely chopped. Scrape the mixture into a large bowl. Add the turkey, bread crumbs, egg, mayonnaise, and a big pinch of salt and pepper. Use your hands to mix until combined, being careful not to overwork the meat.

Use a ¼ cup [60 g] measure to scoop the meat and roll into balls. Arrange half of the meatballs on each prepared baking sheet. Bake the meatballs for 20 to 25 minutes, turning and swapping the baking sheets halfway, until cooked through and golden brown. Serve immediately or let cool and then refrigerate in an airtight container for up to 1 week.

PPS

{PEPPERS, POTATOES, SAUSAGE}

SERVES / **4 TO 6**

4 russet potatoes (about 2½ lb [1.1 kg]), peeled, halved lengthwise, and cut into ½ in [13 mm] thick slices

2 green bell peppers, cut into 1 in [2.5 cm] strips

2 white onions, halved and cut into ½ in [13 mm] thick slices

¼ cup [60 g] extra-virgin olive oil

Kosher salt and freshly ground black pepper

1 lb [455 g] Italian sausage, sweet or hot, cut into 2 in [5 cm] pieces

This is the holy grail of Italian American cooking. It's a crowd-pleaser, it's cheap, it's easy to make on the fly, and it's probably the most requested thing in my household. My children, husband, nieces, nephews, cousins, and siblings all demand it when they walk through the door. It's a simple combo, but I say when something works, don't mess with it. It's great hot out of the oven, when the sausage fat has seeped into the vegetables. But it's even better the next day, reheated with eggs or stuffed cold into subs.

Preheat the oven to 375°F [190°C]. Line a rimmed baking sheet with aluminum foil.

In a large pot, combine the potato slices and enough cold salted water to cover. Set over high heat and bring to a boil. Parboil the potatoes for 5 minutes, until starting to soften but still firm. Drain the potatoes and let cool slightly.

On the prepared baking sheet, toss the peppers, onions, potatoes, olive oil, and a couple big pinches of salt and pepper. Nestle the sausage among the veggies. Cover the baking sheet with more foil and bake for 30 minutes, until the vegetables are tender and the sausage is cooked through. Increase the temperature to 425°F [220°C] and discard the foil. Bake for about 10 minutes longer, until everything is nicely browned. Serve immediately.

SUNDAY *Gravy*

SERVES / **8 TO 10**

¼ cup [60 ml] extra-virgin olive oil

1 recipe Slow-Braised Braciole (page 136)

1 recipe Manzo Meatballs (page 139) (optional)

2 lb [910 g] hot or sweet Italian sausage (I like a mix of both)

3 veal bones (see Note)

3 pork bones (see Note)

8 garlic cloves, crushed

1 small white onion, diced

Three 28 oz [795 g] cans whole peeled tomatoes, broken up

Two 6 oz [170 g] cans tomato paste

1½ cups [360 ml] red wine

Large handful of fresh basil leaves

Kosher salt and freshly ground black pepper

Parmesan cheese and crusty bread, for serving

Is it gravy or is it sauce? We'll probably never agree on that. But whatever you call it, we can all agree this is what Sunday smells like in an Italian American kitchen. To this day, having my own pot of gravy bubbling away will always transport me back to my childhood. I can see my family moving around the kitchen in perfect choreography, hear the voices of everyone entering the house for dinner. I used to excitedly help squish the canned tomatoes with my hands, probably my earliest introduction to cooking. Sunday is the day when everyone can be Italian. It's the day everyone is at the table, everyone gathers, and everyone eats. And no Sunday is complete without a big pot of gravy in the center of the table.

In a large pot over medium heat, heat the olive oil. When the oil shimmers, lower in the braciole. Sear on all sides until nicely browned, about 12 minutes total. Remove the braciole to a plate to rest. Add the meatballs (if using) and brown on both sides, about 8 minutes total. Remove to the plate with the braciole. Add the sausage and bones. Brown on both sides, about 6 minutes total. Stir in the garlic and onion until fragrant, about 1 minute.

Immediately add the canned tomatoes and tomato paste and stir until combined. Nestle the braciole and meatballs into the pot and pour in any juices from the plate. Simmer for 10 to 15 minutes to meld the flavors. When the gravy begins to bubble, turn the heat to low. Stir in the wine, basil leaves, and a couple good pinches of salt and pepper. Keep the gravy simmering on low, stirring occasionally, until fragrant, thick, and flavorful, 2½ to 3 hours.

Remove from the heat. Transfer the braciole to a cutting board, discard the string or toothpicks, thinly slice, and arrange on a serving platter. Remove the sausages, slice, and add to the platter. Remove the bones and discard. Spoon some of the gravy over the meat and leave the rest in the pot. Serve immediately with a hunk of cheese for grating and plenty of bread for dipping.

 Most grocery store meat counters will be able to sell you bones. Neck bones are my preference, but any small bones, like spareribs, side bones, or any soup bones, will work. If you can't find veal bones, just double up on pork bones.

Bolognese

- 1 white onion, roughly chopped
- 1 celery stalk, roughly chopped
- 1 medium carrot, roughly chopped
- 2 garlic cloves, smashed
- 1/4 cup [60 ml] extra-virgin olive oil
- 8 oz [230 g] ground beef
- 8 oz [230 g] ground pork or veal
- Kosher salt and freshly ground black pepper
- 1 cup [240 ml] red wine
- 1 cup [240 ml] chicken stock
- 1 cup [240 ml] whole milk
- One 28 oz [795 g] can crushed tomatoes
- 1 Tbsp finely chopped fresh basil
- 2 tsp fresh oregano leaves
- 4 Tbsp [55 g] unsalted butter

◆◆◆◆◆◆◆◆◆◆◆◆◆◆◆◆◆◆◆◆◆◆◆◆

In my house, everyone expects the hearty Sunday Gravy (facing page) to be on the table every Sunday. But after a while, I need a break from the heavy eating and piles of rich meats. When I want all the comfort, smells, and flavors with a slightly lighter touch, I make a big batch of Bolognese. This sauce is still hearty and filling, and it smells incredible simmering away on the stove for hours. But the real win here is using it as leftovers. The sauce can swirl on a pizza, get covered with mashed potatoes like a shepherd's pie, or be the filling for Deep-Dish Sausage Pizza Pie (page 84).

◆◆◆◆◆◆◆◆◆◆◆◆◆◆◆◆◆◆◆◆◆◆◆◆

In a food processor, combine the onion, celery, carrot, and garlic. Pulse about six times until the veggies are finely chopped.

In a large saucepan over medium heat, heat the olive oil. When the oil shimmers, add the veggies. Sauté, stirring often, until the veggies are vibrant and fragrant, about 2 minutes. Add the beef, pork, and a good pinch of salt and pepper. Use a wooden spoon to break up the meat as it browns, about 5 minutes.

Stir in the red wine. Simmer, using the wooden spoon to continue breaking the meat into tiny pieces, until the wine is almost completely evaporated, about 10 minutes. Stir in the chicken stock, milk, tomatoes, basil, oregano, and another big pinch of salt and pepper. Bring to a simmer, then turn the heat to low. Simmer, stirring occasionally, until the meat is very tender and the sauce is rich and nicely thick, about 3 hours. Just before serving, add the butter and stir until completely melted and incorporated into a glossy sauce. Leftover Bolognese can be refrigerated in an airtight container for up to 5 days or frozen for up to 3 months.

 Use the Bolognese on its own, or serve over fettuccine with Parmesan for grating. For every 1 lb [455 g] of pasta, use 2 cups [480 ml] of Bolognese and toss with about 1/4 cup [60 ml] of the pasta cooking water to evenly coat the noodles.

Home for the Holidays

....

If I have fifty people over on Christmas Eve, it means it was a slow year. Seriously. We go big, and that includes the food! If you're in my home for the holidays, you're leaving with lots of good cheer and an armful of leftovers.

ORANGE & FENNEL *Salad*

SERVES / **4 TO 6**

3 blood oranges

3 navel oranges

1 large red onion, thinly sliced

1 large fennel bulb, cored, thinly sliced, and fronds reserved

2 Tbsp extra-virgin olive oil

Kosher salt and freshly ground black pepper

◆◆◆◆◆◆◆◆◆◆◆◆◆◆◆◆◆◆◆◆◆◆◆◆◆

I always serve this light, refreshing side during the holidays, when we're at our peak of heavy eating. But really, it would be perfect any time of year. The tart oranges are a perfect flavor pairing with fennel, which is also great for digestion. (Fennel doesn't get enough credit as a vegetable.) The important thing is to finish with a really good olive oil—not the one you use for cooking, but the secret bottle you keep stashed away.

◆◆◆◆◆◆◆◆◆◆◆◆◆◆◆◆◆◆◆◆◆◆◆◆◆

To peel the oranges, cut a small slice from the top and the bottom of the citrus so you have a clear view of the fruit inside. Set the citrus on one of the flat sides and run your knife from top to bottom, following the curve of the fruit. The goal is to remove the peel and white pith, but ideally not too much fruit. Rotate the fruit as you slice away small sections. Once the oranges are peeled, cut into ½ in [13 mm] thick rounds.

In a large bowl, gently toss the orange rounds, onion, fennel, olive oil, and a couple big pinches of salt and pepper until combined. Arrange on a serving platter and finish with a sprinkling of fennel fronds and a little more black pepper.

HAZELNUT & BEET *Salad*

SERVES / 4

I love beets. If they're on a menu, if they're in the grocery, you can bet I'm getting the beets. My other favorite thing, hazelnuts, is an ideal partner, balancing things out with a toasty crunch. I make this salad all the time and keep it in the fridge as a snack for myself. But during the holidays, I roll it out as a vibrant and beautiful side. It immediately makes the table look more festive and put together.

- 1 lb [455 g] red or yellow beets, scrubbed
- 3 Tbsp extra-virgin olive oil
- 2 Tbsp red wine vinegar
- 1 tsp kosher salt
- 1/2 tsp freshly ground black pepper
- 1/4 cup [30 g] whole hazelnuts

In a medium saucepan, combine the beets and enough water to cover. Set over high heat and bring to a boil. Turn the heat to medium and simmer until a paring knife easily slides in and out of a beet, about 40 minutes. Drain the beets and let cool for about 10 minutes, or until cool enough to handle. Peel the beets and cut in half. Chop into 1/4 in [6 mm] thick slices. I highly recommend wearing gloves while handling the beets.

In a medium bowl, toss the warm beets with the olive oil, vinegar, salt, and pepper. Cover with plastic wrap and refrigerate for 2 hours, until cool, or overnight.

Just before serving, heat a small skillet over medium heat. Add the hazelnuts and toss occasionally until fragrant and toasted, about 4 minutes. Remove to a cutting board and roughly chop.

Transfer the beets and dressing to a serving platter and garnish with the hazelnuts before serving.

ORANGE &
FENNEL SALAD
PAGE 148

ANTIPASTI
SPREAD
PAGE 153

STUFFED
MUSHROOMS
PAGE 152

HAZELNUT &
BEET SALAD
PAGE 149

WHIPPED
CANNELLINI &
HERB CROSTINI
PAGE 154

Stuffed MUSHROOMS

SERVES / 4 TO 6

12 baby bella or white button mushrooms

¼ cup [3 g] fresh parsley leaves

2 Tbsp extra-virgin olive oil

2 medium white onions, diced

5 garlic cloves, minced

1 cup [240 ml] chicken stock

½ cup [120 ml] dry white wine

6 Tbsp [85 g] unsalted butter

1 cup [140 g] seasoned bread crumbs

½ cup [30 g] grated pecorino cheese

Kosher salt and freshly ground black pepper

To me, stuffed mushrooms make December feel like Christmas. Growing up, they were a tradition in my family, something I looked forward to all year, to nibbling on the savory, crispy filling. (I was probably less excited about the mushroom part.) Every year, I make these around the holidays. I guess that's just stuck in my bones, and I can't make them any other time of the year!

Preheat the oven to 350°F [180°C]. Line a rimmed baking sheet with aluminum foil and rub with olive oil.

Remove and reserve the mushroom stems. Using a small spoon, hollow out the mushroom caps and reserve the innards. Arrange the caps on the prepared baking sheet and set aside.

In a food processor, add the parsley, mushroom stems, and innards and pulse about six times until broken down.

In a large skillet over low heat, heat the olive oil. When the oil shimmers, add the onion and garlic and sauté until translucent and very fragrant, about 5 minutes. Add the mushroom mixture and sauté until soft, about 5 minutes. Add the stock, wine, and 4 Tbsp [55 g] of the butter. Simmer until reduced slightly, about 5 minutes, then stir in the bread crumbs and pecorino. Continue to simmer, stirring occasionally, until the mixture forms a thick paste, about 3 more minutes. Season with a good pinch of salt and pepper.

Cut the remaining 2 Tbsp of butter into twelve pieces. Divide the mixture among the mushroom caps and place a piece of butter over the filling. Bake for 30 minutes, until the mushrooms are soft. Set the broiler to high. Slide the baking sheet under the broiler and broil for 3 to 5 minutes until the filling is golden brown and crispy. Serve warm.

Antipasti SPREAD

Instead of a strict recipe, I want to give you a guide to making your own antipasti spread. To me, antipasti is life. I wouldn't dare invite anyone over if there's not antipasti ready to go. It's what brings us together in the kitchen, gathers everyone around, and gets the conversation going. But I do put the antipasti way at the far end of the kitchen counter, far enough to keep them away from me so I can work, but still close enough so I can talk to everyone. There are no hard-and-fast rules to building your spread, but a few key points of advice that I'll outline below. The important thing is to be flexible to the size of your crowd, build in a variety of flavors and textures, and make it look nice but not so nice that no one wants to touch it. I used to run the show, but in recent years my daughter, Lauren, and daughter-in-law, Chelsea, have become the queens of the antipasti. I taught them everything I know, so now I can just buy the ingredients and leave them to make it look pretty.

FIRST, ARRANGE YOUR CHEESES across the board with bowls of honey or jam to accompany. Make sure the cheeses are a mixture of hard (pecorino, Parmesan, or Asiago), semisoft (fontina, Taleggio, or provolone), soft (Gorgonzola, caprino, or scamorza), and fresh (Burrata, stracciatella, or ricotta). Assume 2 to 4 oz [55 to 115 g] of cheese per guest.

NEXT, CREATE POCKETS OF CURED MEATS, like prosciutto, speck, bresaola, salami, or capicola. Assume 2 to 4 oz [55 to 115 g] of meat per guest.

START FILLING IN THE BOARD with a mix of fruit, like fresh apples, pears, figs, and oranges, plus dried apricots, dates, prunes, and cherries. Big bunches of grapes are always a good idea. Then it's time for pockets of nuts, like almonds (Marcona almonds are my favorite), pistachios, walnuts, and hazelnuts.

GET YOUR CARBS IN ORDER. Mix softer things like sliced ciabatta or focaccia alongside crackers or grissini. Fill in the missing areas with olives, pepperoncini, pickled or marinated vegetables, spreads, dips, or small plates.

SOME ANTIPASTI OPTIONS from this book include Tapenade (page 36), Long Hots (page 37), Baked Tomatoes (page 38), Roasted Red Peppers (page 39), Garlic Bread (page 41), Grilled Artichokes with Lemon Aioli (page 92), Burrata with Prosciutto & Red Peppers (page 123), Manzo Meatballs (page 139), Orange & Fennel Salad (page 148), Hazelnut & Beet Salad (page 149), Stuffed Mushrooms (facing page), or Homemade Crostini with Four Bruschetta (page 154). All of them would be delicious, but none of them is required.

FINALLY, IT'S TIME TO MAKE IT INVITING. Make sure the fruit is sliced. Arrange knives with each cheese and cut off the first few pieces. Make sure anything that needs a small serving fork, spoon, or knife has one close by. Mess up a few pieces of meat or scatter the nuts a little out of their zone. Make it look like someone has already started snacking so no one feels shy to kick things off. Add a stack of small plates and napkins within reach and serve with plenty of wine to get the party flowing.

HOMEMADE *Crostini*
WITH FOUR BRUSCHETTA

MAKES / **ABOUT 60 PIECES**

I make crostini a billion different ways, reinventing the wheel over and over again. They're the perfect blank canvas to use up stale bread or raid the fridge for anything that can be passed off as a new invention. They're great as part of an Antipasti Spread (page 153), or they can stand alone when you need a simple appetizer without pulling out all the stops. Here are four of my favorite go-tos. You can spend time really making these pretty, or just throw them together and serve them rustic style. Either way, they're delicious.

CROSTINI

1 baguette or other crusty bread, such as ciabatta, cut into 1/4 in [6 mm] thick slices

Extra-virgin olive oil, for brushing

Kosher salt and freshly ground black pepper

Preheat the oven to 375°F [190°C].

TO MAKE THE CROSTINI: Brush the slices of bread on both sides with olive oil and season lightly with salt and pepper. Arrange on a baking sheet, working in batches if needed. Bake for 12 to 15 minutes, flipping the crostini halfway through, until golden and crisp. Serve hot, warm, or at room temperature.

RICOTTA & HONEY

2 cups [480 g] ricotta cheese

Zest of 1 lemon

1/2 tsp kosher salt

1/2 tsp freshly ground black pepper, very coarse grind

Honey and sliced almonds, for serving

In a small bowl, mix the ricotta, lemon zest, salt, and pepper.

Spread the ricotta mixture over each crostino, about 1½ tsp each. Drizzle with honey and top with sliced almonds before serving.

CUCUMBER & DILL

Two 8 oz [230 g] packages cream cheese, at room temperature

1 Tbsp whole milk

1/4 cup [10 g] finely chopped fresh dill, plus whole fronds for garnish

3 Persian cucumbers, cut into 1/4 in [6 mm] thick slices

Kosher salt and freshly ground black pepper

In a small bowl, mix the cream cheese, milk, and dill. Spread a thin layer of the cream cheese mixture over each crostino, about 1½ tsp each. Arrange two cucumber slices on each and season lightly with salt and pepper. Finish with a dill frond for garnish.

WHIPPED CANNELLINI & HERBS

One 15.5 oz [440 g] can cannellini beans, rinsed and drained

2 Tbsp extra-virgin olive oil

Juice of 1 lemon

1 garlic clove

1/2 tsp kosher salt

1/2 tsp freshly ground black pepper, plus more for serving

1 ice cube

2 Tbsp finely chopped fresh herbs, such as rosemary, thyme, sage, or a combination

In a food processor, combine the beans, olive oil, lemon juice, garlic, salt, pepper, and ice cube. Process until smooth, about 2 minutes.

Spread the bean mixture over each crostino, about 1½ tsp each. Sprinkle with herbs and finish with black pepper before serving.

NOTE: The ice cube gives the spread a super creamy texture!

BRIE & TOMATO

One 7 oz [200 g] jar sun-dried tomatoes

8 oz [230 g] Brie cheese, thinly sliced

Kosher salt and freshly ground black pepper

Drain the tomatoes, reserving the oil, and roughly chop. Arrange a slice of Brie and a small pile of tomatoes on each crostino. Season lightly with salt and pepper, then spoon on a little of the reserved oil before serving.

SNOW DAY
HOMEMADE *Pasta*

MAKES / ABOUT 2 LB [910 G]

◆◆◆◆◆◆◆◆◆◆◆◆◆◆◆◆◆◆◆◆◆◆◆◆◆◆◆◆◆◆◆◆

A few times every winter, when a big snowstorm hit and the kids were home from school, I would treat my family to homemade pasta. There's nothing hard about making pasta by hand; it's just the type of project that needs a full afternoon. Kneading the dough takes a little elbow grease, and maybe a couple of breaks. But rolling the dough into sheets is the perfect project for a house of restless kids. The most important ingredient in making pasta is patience. Rolling each sheet little by little forces you to slow down and commit to the process. (It can actually be kind of meditative.) But taking the time to get it right pays off with springy, chewy pasta that you just can't get in a box.

◆◆◆◆◆◆◆◆◆◆◆◆◆◆◆◆◆◆◆◆◆◆◆◆◆◆◆◆◆◆◆◆

2 cups [280 g] all-purpose
flour, plus more as needed

2 cups [280 g] 00 flour
(see Note, page 159)

4 eggs

Mound the flour in the center of a large wooden board or clean counter. Use your hand to make a well in the center of the flour and add the eggs. Use a fork to beat the eggs together and then begin to pull in the flour, starting with the inner rim of the well. Keep beating and pulling in more flour, pushing up the outer edges of flour to keep the well shape. It's going to all look messy, and that's the point!

When about half of the flour is incorporated, the dough will start to come together. Ditch the fork and use the palms of your hands to start kneading the dough together. Once the dough is a cohesive mass, set aside and scrape up and discard any dried bits stuck to the surface.

Continue kneading the dough for about 10 minutes, wetting your hands or dusting the surface with more flour as needed, until the dough is elastic and slightly sticky. Wrap in plastic and let rest for 30 minutes at room temperature before using. The dough can also be refrigerated for up to 24 hours. Bring to room temperature before rolling.

A GUIDE TO
Rolling Pasta

1 Generously coat a rimmed baking sheet with flour. Cut the dough into eight equal portions and arrange on the baking sheet. Dust with more flour, then cover with a kitchen towel so the dough doesn't dry out.

2 Take one portion of dough and use your hands to flatten it into a thick disk. Send it through a pasta roller on the thickest setting (that's usually 1, but refer to your machine's directions) two or three times until it's a long rectangle. Fold in thirds like a letter and send it through a few more times, doing the letter fold each time. (This develops the gluten for springy pasta.)

3 Work your way up through the settings one at a time, sending the pasta through twice before moving on to the next setting. (No need to do the letter fold here.) If the pasta sheet gets too long, cut it in half and continue rolling. Just don't forget what setting you have to go back to for the other half!

4 When the pasta is at the desired thickness, switch to the cutter attachment. Add ¼ cup [35 g] of flour to a medium bowl and set the bowl under the cutter. Feed the pasta sheet through so the cut pasta falls into the bowl. Toss to coat in the flour, then wrap the noodles around your hand to create a bundle. Set the bundle on the floured baking sheet with the dough and cover with the kitchen towel while rolling out the rest.

PASTA CAN BE ROLLED BY HAND with a rolling pin on a well-floured surface. Follow the rolling and folding step, lifting the pasta occasionally to make sure it's not sticking and adding flour as needed. Continue rolling the pasta to the desired thinness, then dust the surface of the sheet with flour and roll in up. Use a knife to slice into noodles, then toss with flour and store while rolling the rest.

TO FREEZE THE PASTA, transfer the bundles to a clean baking sheet lined with parchment. Freeze overnight, then transfer the bundles to a freezer bag. The pasta is best used within a month or two, but it can last for up to 3 months. It can be dropped directly into boiling water; just add an extra minute of cooking time.

PASTA CAN BE COOKED IMMEDIATELY in boiling salted water. Depending on the thickness, the pasta will be ready to be tossed in sauce after boiling for 1 to 3 minutes. Add an extra minute for frozen pasta.

NOTE: The 00 flour is a finely ground flour commonly used in Italy for pasta and pizza dough. If you can't find it in your grocery store, just use 2 more cups [280 g] of all-purpose flour instead.

PASTA
WITH
Olive Sauce

SERVES / 8

4 oz [115 g] pancetta, cubed

4 oz [115 g] thinly sliced prosciutto, roughly chopped

6 oz [170 g] cured salami, roughly chopped

1 white onion, diced

4 garlic cloves, minced

Red pepper flakes

One 3.5 oz [100 g] jar nonpareil capers

Two 8 oz [230 g] jars pitted olives, any variety

One 14.5 oz [410 g] can chicken stock

One 28 oz [795 g] can whole peeled tomatoes

Kosher salt and freshly ground black pepper

1 lb [455 g] dried pasta (I use fusilli, but any type works)

This olive sauce was an invention of my dad's, made on the fly. Growing up, we would shuttle between Queens and our farm upstate. This one time, we hadn't been up there in a few months, so the cupboards were empty except for a few scattered things like a jar of capers, some red pepper flakes, a couple jars of olives, and cans of chicken broth and tomatoes. My mom always kept us kids quiet on the drive with a bunch of snacks, so we had slices of salami and prosciutto on hand. So my dad, who was a pro at making something out of nothing, just grabbed everything and decided to whip up a sauce. It might sound like an unlikely mix, but trust me, it's so good, it's criminal. It immediately became a staple and my family has been making this olive sauce for more than fifty years. I make it every year, only on Christmas Eve, as a special tribute, in memory of my dad. When it hits the table, I can feel that he's there with us.

In a Dutch oven, spread the pancetta in an even layer. Set over medium heat and let the fat start to render. Once the pancetta is sizzling, add the prosciutto, salami, onion, garlic, and a pinch of red pepper flakes. Sauté until the onion is translucent and the pancetta is crisp, about 5 minutes.

Stir in the capers with their brine, olives with their brine, chicken stock, tomatoes, and a small pinch of salt and black pepper. Bring to a boil, then turn the heat to low. Simmer for 2 to 3 hours, using a wooden spoon to break up the tomatoes and olives a bit, until the sauce is reduced and nicely thick. Taste for seasoning.

Just before serving, bring a large pot of salted water to a boil over high heat. Cook the pasta to al dente according to the package directions. Drain the pasta, then add it to the sauce. Stir to thoroughly coat the pasta and serve directly from the pot.

Don't microwave leftover pasta! Add it to a skillet with a splash of water, set over medium heat, and toss until warmed through.

Frangelico
BAKED SWEET POTATOES
WITH MASCARPONE

SERVES / 6 TO 8

6 medium sweet potatoes, scrubbed

Kosher salt and freshly ground black pepper

½ cup [113 g] unsalted butter

2 shallots, diced

1½ cups [210 g] hazelnuts, roughly chopped

2 oz [60 ml] Frangelico liqueur

2 or 3 fresh rosemary sprigs

1 recipe Frangelico Mascarpone Topping (recipe follows)

I've always loved candied sweet potatoes, but I wanted to find a way to pump them up when Rachael Ray invited me on her show to make Thanksgiving dinner. The hazelnut notes of Frangelico are perfect for infusing the sweet potatoes with lots of flavor. And instead of marshmallows, I decided to spoon over a mascarpone topping spiked with more Frangelico. These are sweet potatoes done right!

Preheat the oven to 375°F [190°C].

Lay a pair of wooden spoons, about even in height, parallel to each other. Nestle a sweet potato between the spoon handles. Make four or five slices across the width of the potato, letting the spoons stop your knife from cutting all the way through. Arrange the sliced potatoes in a large oven-safe skillet and season well with salt and pepper.

In a small saucepan over medium heat, melt the butter. Add the shallots and hazelnuts. Sauté, stirring occasionally, until the shallots soften, about 4 minutes. Add the Frangelico and let it cook off for about 2 minutes. Spoon the sauce over the sweet potatoes and nestle the rosemary sprigs around the skillet.

Cover the skillet with aluminum foil and bake for 40 to 60 minutes, until a fork easily pierces the potato. Add a splash of water to the skillet if the liquid is cooking off too fast. Remove the foil and continue to bake for about 10 minutes, until the hazelnuts and potatoes brown slightly.

Remove from the oven and spoon the Frangelico mascarpone topping over the potatoes and around the skillet. Serve directly from the skillet.

FRANGELICO MASCARPONE TOPPING

MAKES ABOUT
1¼ CUPS [300 ML]

4 Tbsp [55 g] unsalted butter
2 oz [60 ml] Frangelico liqueur
1 tsp ground cinnamon
8 oz [230 g] mascarpone cheese

In a small skillet over low heat, melt the butter. Add the Frangelico and cinnamon and whisk until completely combined. Remove from the heat and add the mascarpone. Whisk as it melts until the sauce is combined. Serve warm.

Baked
MACARONI
& CHEESE

SERVES / 8

8 Tbsp [113 g] unsalted butter

1 large white onion, diced

6 Tbsp [60 g] all-purpose flour

1 Tbsp spicy brown mustard

1 tsp mustard powder

1½ tsp kosher salt

½ tsp white pepper

3 cups [720 ml] whole milk

1 lb [455 g] sharp Cheddar
  cheese, finely shredded
  (about 4 cups)

1 lb [455 g] dried elbow
  macaroni

½ cup [70 g] bread crumbs

This is cold weather comfort food at its best. It's always a side on my Thanksgiving table and a guaranteed crowd pleaser for all—my kids love it, my granddaughter loves it, my husband loves it. And while I love a shortcut in cooking, mac and cheese is one thing where I think it's a crime to do it any other way than homemade. But that doesn't mean you have to be fussy with it—sometimes I don't even bother baking it, I just serve right out of the pot, hot and gooey. During the holidays, when my kids are out all night with their friends, I like to leave a pan of mac and cheese out on the counter for when they come stumbling in hungry.

Preheat the oven to 375°F [190°C]. Coat a 9 by 13 in [23 by 33 cm] baking dish with nonstick spray.

In a large saucepan over medium heat, melt 6 Tbsp [85 g] of the butter. Add the onions and sauté until translucent, about 5 minutes. Sprinkle the flour over the onions and stir until the mixture thickens and turns lightly golden, about 3 minutes. Stir in the brown mustard, mustard powder, salt, and white pepper. Pour in the milk and stir until the flour mixture dissolves and starts to thicken, about 6 minutes. Add the cheese and stir until melted and smooth, about 2 minutes. Remove from the heat.

Bring a large pot of salted water to a boil over high heat. Cook the macaroni to al dente according to the package directions. Drain the pasta, then add it back to the same pot off the heat. Scrape the cheese sauce into the pot and stir to thoroughly coat the pasta. Transfer everything to the prepared baking dish.

In a small microwave-safe bowl, melt the remaining 2 Tbsp of butter. Add the bread crumbs and toss to coat. Sprinkle the bread crumbs over the macaroni. Bake for 20 to 30 minutes until the topping is golden brown and the sauce is bubbly. Serve immediately.

Thanksgiving STUFFING

SERVES / 8 TO 10

I have to admit something. I have never made a Thanksgiving turkey. There's really no point when the Brownstone, my husband's catering company, churns out hundreds every Thanksgiving and Al can easily bring one home with him. If there's a shortcut, I'm going to take it! Where I don't cut corners is a simple, classic stuffing done well. Because I'm not stuffing and roasting my own bird, I make my stuffing as a side, which lets me control the flavor and consistency better anyway. This is my Thanksgiving masterpiece, and it's what everyone asks for when they come over.

1 lb [455 g] loaf Italian bread, cut into 1/2 in [13 mm] cubes

1/2 cup [113 g] unsalted butter

1 white onion, diced

4 garlic cloves, minced

1 lb [455 g] sweet Italian sausage, casings removed

1 cup [240 ml] chicken broth

1 cup [240 ml] dry white wine

1 Tbsp fresh thyme leaves

1 Tbsp finely chopped fresh sage

Kosher salt and freshly ground black pepper

1/2 cup [30 g] grated pecorino or 1/2 cup [15 g] Parmesan cheese

2 Tbsp finely chopped fresh parsley

Preheat the oven to 350°F [180°C].

On a rimmed baking sheet, spread the bread cubes in an even layer. Toast in the oven for 20 to 30 minutes, until crisp but not overly browned. Transfer the bread to a 9 by 13 in [23 by 33 cm] baking pan.

In a large skillet over medium heat, melt the butter. Add the onion and garlic and sauté until translucent and very fragrant, about 5 minutes. Add the sausage and use a wooden spoon to break it up as it browns, about 5 minutes. Add the broth, wine, thyme, sage, and a good pinch of salt and pepper to the skillet and stir to combine. As soon as the mixture comes to a simmer, remove from the heat.

Sprinkle the cheese all over the bread cubes, then pour the contents of the skillet evenly over the baking pan. Cover the pan with aluminum foil and bake for about 15 minutes, until the bread is swollen. Discard the foil and stir the stuffing to mix everything together. Bake for about 10 more minutes, until the top is toasted and crispy. Garnish with the parsley and serve immediately.

N·O·T·E

If you don't want to go through the trouble of cutting up bread, just grab one of those big bags of cubed stuffing. Sometimes I even use a mix of the bag stuffing and the fresh bread to boost the flavors!

Extreme
MASHED
POTATOES

(SERVES / 8)

Years ago, Rachael Ray asked me to be on her show for a Thanksgiving episode. I wanted to give her something original, so I came up with this recipe as a way to turbocharge simple mashed potatoes. Be warned, this is not for the faint of heart. It's rich and fatty and hearty, but oh my god is it incredible. Save it for the holidays when it's the perfect time to indulge.

2 lb [910 g] russet potatoes, peeled and diced

1/2 cup [113 g] unsalted butter

1 large white onion, diced

4 pieces thinly sliced prosciutto, roughly chopped

4 sprigs fresh sage leaves, chopped (optional)

1 cup [240 ml] whole milk

1/4 cup [60 ml] half-and-half

8 oz [230 g] mozzarella cheese, cubed (preferably whole milk, low-moisture mozzarella for a great cheese pull)

1/2 cup [30 g] grated pecorino cheese

1 Tbsp finely chopped fresh parsley

Kosher salt and freshly ground black pepper

In a large pot, combine the potatoes and enough cold salted water to cover. Set over medium heat and bring to a simmer. Cook until the potatoes can be easily pierced with a fork, 15 to 20 minutes. Drain the potatoes. Transfer the potatoes back to the pot and mash. (For an extra smooth mash, use a ricer instead.)

While the potatoes are cooking, in a medium saucepan over medium heat, melt the butter. Add the onion, prosciutto, and sage (if using). Sauté, stirring occasionally, until the onion is translucent and the prosciutto is crisp, about 5 minutes. Stir in the milk and half-and-half. Warm the mixture until a few bubbles just start to break the surface. Remove from the heat.

Once the potatoes are mashed, return the pot to low heat. Fold in the mozzarella, pecorino, parsley, and a few big pinches of salt and pepper. Fold in half of the milk mixture, then add the rest and fold until combined.

The mashed potatoes are ready to be served, but if you really want to take it to the extreme: Set the broiler to high. Slide the pot under the broiler and broil for 1 to 3 minutes, until the top is deeply golden brown. Serve straight from the pot.

15-MINUTE Pot Pie

(SERVES / **4 TO 6**)

One 16 oz [455 g] bag frozen mixed vegetables

One 10.75 oz [305 g] can cream of mushroom soup

2/3 cup [160 ml] whole milk

2 cups [280 g] diced leftover turkey meat or 2 cooked chicken breasts, diced

Two 9 in [23 cm] frozen pie crusts, thawed

◆◆◆◆◆◆◆◆◆◆◆◆◆◆◆◆◆◆◆◆◆◆◆◆◆

That is the coup of the century! People will think you worked away on this all day, but it only takes 15 minutes and it's stupidly good. This was a recipe my mother-in-law used to make with leftover turkey the day after Thanksgiving. I was totally in the dark on the magic of this recipe until one day she pulled me into the kitchen to teach me the secret. Now it's one of my all-time favorites, either after Thanksgiving or as a chicken pot pie the rest of the year. You will fool everyone and their mother with the homemade taste.

◆◆◆◆◆◆◆◆◆◆◆◆◆◆◆◆◆◆◆◆◆◆◆◆◆

Preheat the oven to 350°F [180°C].

In a large bowl, combine the frozen vegetables and cream of mushroom soup. Fill the empty can halfway with the milk, give it a swirl, and add it to the bowl, along with the turkey meat. Mix well with a wooden spoon.

Pour the mixture into one of the pie crusts and spread in an even layer. Remove the other pie crust from its foil pie plate and lay it on top to cover, then crimp the edges with your fingers or the tines of a fork. Use a knife or fork to poke vent holes in the top crust. Set the pie on a rimmed baking sheet as safety for a spillover. Bake for about 45 minutes until the crust is golden brown. Remove from the oven and let the pie set for 10 minutes before slicing and serving.

Perfect LEMON CHICKEN

SERVES 4

This is inspired by one of my favorite dishes at Rao's, the mecca for Italian food in Manhattan. After eating it for years, I got in the kitchen and started working on my version, changing a few things along the way. When you need to feed a crowd, this is an easy way out. I just multiply the base recipe, loading up one baking sheet after another, and sliding them in and out of the oven. If I need to bulk it up, I treat it like the PPS (page 143), skipping the sausage but parboiling the potatoes and adding the veggies to the sheet. From there you can just broil the chicken as usual, and you instantly have a main and a side all in one! Just remember to always serve it with lots of bread to catch all the delicious pan juices.

1 whole chicken (4 to 6 lb [1.8 to 2.7 kg]), cut into parts

Kosher salt

1 cup [240 ml] fresh lemon juice

½ cup [120 ml] extra-virgin olive oil

1 Tbsp red wine vinegar

4 garlic cloves, minced

½ tsp dried oregano

1 Tbsp finely chopped fresh parsley

Red pepper flakes

Crusty bread, for serving

Set the broiler to high. Line a rimmed baking sheet with aluminum foil.

Pat the chicken pieces dry with paper towels and season generously with salt. Arrange on the prepared baking sheet, skin-side up, in an even layer. Slide the sheet under the broiler for 10 minutes, rotating the sheet halfway through. Remove the sheet and flip the pieces skin-side down. Broil for 10 more minutes, rotating the sheet halfway through.

While the chicken broils, make the dressing. In a small bowl, whisk together the lemon juice, olive oil, red wine vinegar, garlic, and oregano.

After the chicken broils on both sides, spoon half of the dressing over the chicken. Slide the sheet under the broiler for 3 minutes. Remove the sheet, flip the chicken skin-side up again, and spoon the remaining half of the dressing over the top. Broil again for 2 to 3 minutes until the skin is perfectly golden brown and the chicken breast has an internal temperature of at least 160°F [71°C].

Remove the chicken pieces to a serving plate to rest. Pour the dressing and any accumulated juices into a small saucepan and set over medium heat. Bring to a simmer and reduce by a third, about 5 minutes. Whisk in the parsley and a small pinch of red pepper flakes. Spoon the sauce over the chicken and serve with crusty bread.

CELEBRATE Every MOMENT

Life's a gift. You don't know what each minute will bring, and you can't count on anything lasting forever. In my lifetime, I've lost family at all different ages, in slow and sudden ways. I've had successes and failures, highs and lows. But it's taught me that every moment is precious and the one thing in life I know for sure is the little things *are* the big things.

When it comes to Italian American culture, family is everything. Our gatherings around the table, filled with laughter and storytelling, are the cornerstone of our identity. We pass down recipes from generation to generation, preserving the essence of our heritage. But it's about more than just the food; it's about celebrating the connections we forge and the memories we create.

So many of my memories revolve around the sounds and smells that bring me back to my childhood, to my parents and grandparents, or to my kids when they were young and discovering the world, fleeting moments I didn't fully appreciate at the time. Life is a whirlwind, small blips in time that create our story. The scent of fresh flowers, the recipes I know by heart, a phone call from my granddaughter, the nonstop crowd blowing through my house around the holidays, or the morning silence of a sleepy vacation house in the summer are all moments of celebration for me.

When my kids were growing up, my husband was working seven days a week. He was breaking his back to create a beautiful life for his family, but he was also missing so many important moments of their childhood that we'd never get back. Al decided he would take one day a week off, and Wednesdays became Daddy Day. He got to join in the celebration of our family, in all the big and small moments of kids growing into adults.

Life isn't always smooth sailing. But in the face of challenges, we discover our strength and resilience. Celebrate the lessons learned from life's trials and find comfort in the growth that comes from them. Celebrate imperfections as part of the unique story that makes you who you are. The bumpy moments shape us and allow us to appreciate the smooth ones.

Every year, during the week between Christmas and New Year's, we go out to dinner as a family, just the core group of Al and me, our kids, and their partners. We splurge on a nice restaurant to mark the year that's behind us and the year ahead of us. Good year, bad year, we're still here! We raise a glass, look into each other's eyes, and celebrate the magic that lives in every moment.

MARINATED

Lamb Chops

SERVES / 4

I love lamb, but it can be expensive. So I save this one for the holidays, when I don't mind spending a little extra on something special. The flavor of these chops is rich and delicious, and letting them marinate overnight really gives you the most bang for your buck. The best part is they sear up quickly, so I multiply the recipe and marinate a big batch (plus a few more than I think I'll need). That way I have the flexibility to make more if a few extra guests show up hungry!

4 garlic cloves, thinly sliced

1 Tbsp finely chopped fresh rosemary

1 Tbsp finely chopped fresh sage

1 Tbsp kosher salt

1 Tbsp freshly ground black pepper

1 cup [240 ml] plus 2 Tbsp extra-virgin olive oil

Eight ½ in [13 mm] thick lamb loin chops

Mix the garlic, rosemary, sage, salt, pepper, and 1 cup [240 ml] of the olive oil in a large zip-top bag. Add the chops, seal the bag, and refrigerate overnight.

In a large skillet over medium-high heat, heat the remaining 2 Tbsp of olive oil. When the oil shimmers, arrange the lamb chops in an even layer (or work in batches). Sear until browned on the bottom, about 3 minutes. Flip the chops and sear for about 2 minutes more for medium-rare. Transfer the chops to plates and serve.

Mussels
MARINARA
WITH
GARLIC BREAD

SERVES / **6 TO 8**

◆◆◆◆◆◆◆◆◆◆◆◆◆◆◆◆◆◆◆◆◆◆◆

Although this makes for a nice, quick main in the summer down the shore, to me this is really a dish that belongs to the winter. I make it in those vague hours between Christmas Eve and Christmas Day, when night is turning into morning, the party has died down, a few people are still lingering, and we need to fill up. For me, it's a marker of time and a special tradition that I share with a treasured few.

◆◆◆◆◆◆◆◆◆◆◆◆◆◆◆◆◆◆◆◆◆◆◆

4 Tbsp [55 g] unsalted butter

2 Tbsp extra-virgin olive oil

4 garlic cloves, thinly sliced

4 plum tomatoes, diced

One 8 oz [230 g] can tomato sauce

1 cup [240 ml] fish or chicken stock

½ cup [120 ml] red wine

Kosher salt

4 lb [1.8 kg] mussels, scrubbed

2 Tbsp finely chopped fresh basil

2 Tbsp finely chopped fresh parsley

Garlic Bread (page 41), for serving

In a Dutch oven over medium heat, melt the butter and oil together. Add the garlic and tomatoes. Sauté, stirring often, until the garlic is lightly browned and the tomatoes are soft, about 4 minutes. Stir in the tomato sauce, stock, wine, and a good pinch of salt. Bring to a simmer and let the liquid reduce by half, about 10 minutes. Add the mussels and cover. Simmer for 5 to 10 minutes, until the mussels have opened. Discard any unopened mussels.

Transfer the mussels and sauce to a large serving bowl. Garnish with the basil and parsley before serving with plenty of garlic bread for dipping.

N·O·T·E

This version has been reduced to feed a small group for dinner. If you're cooking for a crowd, like I usually am, grab a bigger pot and double the recipe.

Something Sweet

◆◆◆◆◆◆◆◆◆

I am not a baker, so if I'm making dessert, it has to be easy. But easy doesn't mean sacrificing elegance, surprise, and— most importantly—deliciousness. Who doesn't love a little something sweet?

Pumpkin
BANANA
"PUDDING"

1/4 cup [30 g] whole hazelnuts

One 15 oz [425 g] can pumpkin purée

One 5.3 oz [150 g] container vanilla Greek yogurt

1 large banana, very ripe, sliced

1/2 tsp ground cinnamon, plus more for garnish

1/4 tsp ground nutmeg

Sometimes getting out of my own kitchen, and my normal routine, is when my most creative cooking happens. This recipe was born at the shore house as a lighter version of pudding. I wish I could say I dreamed it up, but it really was built on instinct based on what I had lying around in the kitchen. It's light and creamy with a perfect sweetness. But most importantly, it's fast, easy, and requires no cooking!

Heat a small skillet over medium heat. Add the hazelnuts and toss occasionally until fragrant and toasted, about 4 minutes. Remove to a cutting board and roughly chop.

In a food processor, combine the pumpkin, yogurt, banana, cinnamon, and nutmeg. Process until everything is combined, about 1 minute. Divide the pudding among serving bowls. Press plastic wrap directly on the surface of each pudding and refrigerate until ready to serve, or up to 2 days.

Garnish with the toasted hazelnuts and a pinch of cinnamon before serving.

Slow Cooker RICE PUDDING

(SERVES / 10)

This easy dessert uses ingredients that I typically have on hand already and is perfect for when I need to feed a huge group. Using the slow cooker means that the rice comes out soft and creamy and the flavors have plenty of time to infuse together. Best of all, I don't need to pay any attention to it. I throw everything in the pot before I start making dinner, and it's ready to go by dessert time, leaving everyone happy and ending the meal on a perfect note.

1¼ cups [250 g] long-grain white rice

½ cup [113 g] unsalted butter, melted

6 cups [1.4 L] whole milk

½ cup [120 ml] heavy cream

1¼ cups [250 g] sugar

1¼ tsp ground cinnamon

1 tsp vanilla extract

Kosher salt

Ground nutmeg

Rinse the rice several times under cold water, until the water runs clear. Drain thoroughly.

Brush the inside of the slow cooker with a little melted butter. In the slow cooker, whisk together the milk, cream, sugar, cinnamon, vanilla, a big pinch of salt, and a small pinch of nutmeg. Stir in the rice and drizzle the melted butter over the top.

Cover and cook on high for 3 to 4 hours, until the rice has absorbed all the liquid. Serve warm straight out of the pot! Any leftover rice pudding can be refrigerated in an airtight container for up to 5 days.

DEEP, DARK CHOCOLATE *Pudding Cake*

SERVES / 8

1 cup [120 g] cake flour

1 1/3 cups [265 g] sugar

1/4 cup [20 g] plus 1/3 cup [25 g] unsweetened cocoa powder

2 tsp baking powder

Kosher salt

1/2 cup [120 ml] whole milk

1 Tbsp vegetable oil

1/2 tsp vanilla extract

1 cup [240 ml] boiling water

Vanilla ice cream, for serving

Ever since I was a kid, we've always had some sort of version of this cake on the table. It's big, rich, decadent, and takes almost no effort to make. The top forms a crust, but the inside stays gooey and sometimes oozes out of the top, so it's a dessert that's meant to be rustic. Sure, you can serve this the polite way, scooping individual portions onto plates and serving with ice cream. Or you can go the Manzo way by plopping a few scoops of ice cream in the center of the pan, handing everyone a spoon, and letting everyone dive to the center of the table and go at it. Either way, you can't go wrong and it'll make everyone happy.

Preheat the oven to 350°F [180°C]. Coat an 8 in [20 cm] cake pan or soufflé dish with nonstick spray.

In a large bowl, whisk together the flour, 2/3 cup [130 g] of the sugar, 1/4 cup [20 g] of the cocoa powder, the baking powder, and a generous pinch of salt. Whisk in the milk, vegetable oil, and vanilla. Scrape the batter into the prepared pan and smooth into an even layer.

In a small bowl, whisk together the remaining 2/3 cup [130 g] of sugar and remaining 1/3 cup [25 g] of cocoa powder. Sprinkle the mixture evenly over the batter. Carefully pour the boiling water over the batter. Do not stir.

Bake for 25 to 30 minutes, until the top of the cake looks dry and a toothpick inserted into the top cake layer comes out clean. (A crust will have formed up top, and underneath the soft pudding layer may pool around the edges.) Let cool in the pan for 5 minutes, then scoop onto plates and serve with a big scoop of ice cream. There will be no leftovers.

NOTE

I love to make a mochaccino version of this cake too. Just add 1/2 tsp of ground cinnamon to the flour mixture and substitute the boiling water with hot extra-strong coffee.

AUNT RED'S *Cheesecake*

SERVES / 10

Aunt Red, my dad's aunt, stood no more than 5 foot 2, but she had a personality that could fill an entire house. She was beloved by the entire family and got her nickname from her flaming red hair. Most importantly, she was a cook like I've never seen in my life. She was my earliest teacher, and my fondest memories are cooking with her at our farmhouse as a kid. This cheesecake is the thing that reminds me the most of her. She would make this seemingly on demand, any time of day, any time of year. It's a perfect cheesecake: dense, rich, creamy, outstanding. This recipe is transcribed directly from her tiny handwriting on a recipe card. I feel so lucky to have this connection to her through one of my very favorite desserts.

CRUST

1 cup [120 g] graham cracker crumbs
  (from 9 graham crackers)

2 Tbsp sugar

½ cup [113 g] unsalted butter, melted

CHEESECAKE

6 eggs, at room temperature

1 cup [200 g] sugar

3 Tbsp all-purpose flour

Two 16 oz [455 g] containers sour cream,
  at room temperature

Three 8 oz [227 g] packages cream cheese,
  at room temperature

1 Tbsp vanilla extract

Preheat the oven to 400°F [200°C].

TO MAKE THE CRUST: In a medium bowl, stir together the graham crackers, sugar, and butter until they look like damp sand. Scrape the mixture into a 9 in [23 cm] springform pan. Use the bottom of a measuring cup to press the crust evenly across the bottom of the pan. Set the pan on a rimmed baking sheet.

TO MAKE THE CHEESECAKE: Separate the egg whites into one large bowl and the yolks into another large bowl. Use a handheld mixer at medium speed to beat the whites to stiff peaks, about 5 minutes.

Add the sugar and flour to the egg yolks and whisk to combine. Add the sour cream, cream cheese, and vanilla and whisk until just combined without adding too much air. Use a rubber spatula to fold in a third of the egg whites to lighten the batter. Slowly fold in the remaining egg whites until fully combined. Gently tap the bowl a few times to bring the air bubbles to the surface. Scrape the batter over the crust in the pan and smooth into an even layer.

Slide the entire baking sheet into the oven and bake for 15 minutes. Without opening the oven door, lower the temperature to 350°F [180°C] and continue baking for 45 to 60 minutes, until the center is just set and the surface is still wobbly. Turn off the heat and barely crack the oven door. Let the cake cool in the oven for 1 hour. Set the cake on a wire rack and let cool for 2 more hours, then loosely cover the top with plastic wrap and refrigerate for at least 4 hours or ideally overnight before serving.

NOTE For a perfectly clean slice, keep a tall glass of hot water and a kitchen towel nearby. Dip the knife in the hot water, then wipe dry on the towel before slicing. Wipe the knife clean, dip in hot water, and dry before each slice.

WAB

{WARM-ASS BROWNIES}

MAKES / 12 BROWNIES

These are my go-to brownies when I have a house full of lazy, lounging family. They're so rich and gooey on the inside, almost a fudgy texture, with bits of melty chocolate chips in every bite. All three of my kids (plus whoever else might be around) absolutely love them, and they always eat them right out of the pan. The name Warm-Ass Brownies started out as a joke, but now we call them WABs for short.

½ cup [113 g] unsalted butter, melted

¼ cup [60 ml] vegetable oil

1 cup [200 g] sugar

½ cup [40 g] unsweetened cocoa powder

2 eggs

1 tsp vanilla extract

1 tsp instant espresso powder (optional)

½ cup [70 g] flour

½ tsp kosher salt

One 12 oz [340 g] bag semisweet chocolate chips

Vanilla ice cream, for serving

Preheat the oven to 350°F [180°C]. Line an 8 by 8 in [20 by 20 cm] baking pan with aluminum foil and coat with nonstick spray.

In a large bowl, whisk together the melted butter, oil, sugar, and cocoa powder. Whisk in the eggs, vanilla, and espresso powder (if using). Sift in the flour and salt. Use a rubber spatula to fold until just a few streaks remain, then fold in the chocolate chips.

Scrape the batter into the prepared baking pan. Bake for 25 to 30 minutes, until a toothpick inserted about 1 in [2.5 cm] from the edge comes out clean (the center will be gooey). Let the brownies cool in the pan for as long as possible, ideally 30 minutes, before cutting into twelve brownies. Serve warm with scoops of ice cream.

ALMOND MACAROON Cookies

MAKES / **ABOUT 24 COOKIES**

2 egg whites

1/4 tsp kosher salt

1 cup [200 g] sugar

1 cup [120 g] ground blanched almonds

1 tsp almond extract

◆◆◆◆◆◆◆◆◆◆◆◆◆◆◆◆◆◆◆◆◆◆◆◆◆◆

The Brownstone, my husband's company, makes the best almond cookies on the planet, but they'll never tell me the recipe. I'm like the shoemaker with the hole in his shoe! After asking for years, I finally gave up and turned to my sister Fran, the baker of the family. She figured out an easy version of the cookie that has a shockingly short ingredients list and is so easy to make. I am no star baker, but these are the kind of cookies I can make over and over and know they'll be perfect every time.

◆◆◆◆◆◆◆◆◆◆◆◆◆◆◆◆◆◆◆◆◆◆◆◆◆◆

Preheat the oven to 325°F [165°C]. Line two rimmed baking sheets with parchment paper.

In a large bowl, use a handheld mixer at medium speed to beat the egg whites and salt until foamy, about 2 minutes. Slowly stream in the sugar and beat to medium peaks, about 3 minutes. Add the almonds and almond extract and beat until combined, about 1 minute.

Use a 1½ Tbsp cookie scoop to scoop the batter. On one baking sheet, drop six rounds with plenty of space between each one. Transfer to the oven and bake for 15 to 20 minutes, until the edges are golden brown and crisp. Let cool on the baking sheet for 5 minutes, then transfer to a wire rack to finish cooling.

Scoop the next batch of six onto the other baking sheet and bake. Continue baking in batches, making sure the baking sheets are completely cooled before using. The cooled cookies can be stored in an airtight container for up to 1 week.

Bow Knot COOKIES

MAKES / **50 COOKIES**

Aunt Red was an incredible cook, but an even better baker. She used to churn out big batches of these knot cookies, which, along with her cheesecake (page 183), were her signature. I lost her recipe for these many years ago, and it still kills me. So this version was cobbled together from my memory of what was on that index card and how I remember them tasting. I have to say, I got pretty close! I only make these once a year, for Christmas, when I have some extra helping hands around, but I love continuing the family tradition that Aunt Red started.

COOKIES

3 cups [420 g] all-purpose flour, plus more for dusting

¾ cup [150 g] granulated sugar

1 Tbsp baking powder

½ cup [113 g] unsalted butter, at room temperature

3 eggs

1 Tbsp sour cream

2 Tbsp anise liqueur or anise extract

½ tsp vanilla extract

GLAZE

1 lb [455 g] confectioners' sugar

8 Tbsp [120 ml] whole milk

1 Tbsp anise liqueur or anise extract

Rainbow nonpareils, for garnish

Preheat the oven to 350°F [180°C]. Line two rimmed baking sheets with parchment paper.

TO MAKE THE COOKIES: In a medium bowl, sift the flour, granulated sugar, and baking powder. In a large bowl, whisk the butter until light and fluffy, about 1 minute. Whisk in the eggs, sour cream, anise liqueur, and vanilla. Add half of the flour mixture and use a wooden spoon to combine. Add the remaining half and knead with your hands to form a soft dough.

Lightly dust a work surface with flour. Pinch off about 2 Tbsp of dough and roll into a 5 in [13 cm] rope. Tie it into a knot and set on one of the prepared baking sheets. Fill the sheet with twelve or thirteen knotted cookies. Bake for 10 to 15 minutes, until the cookies are lightly golden brown and firm. Transfer the cookies to a wire rack to cool completely.

While one batch bakes, roll and shape the next batch onto the other baking sheet. Continue baking in batches, making sure the baking sheets are completely cooled before using.

TO MAKE THE GLAZE: In a medium bowl, whisk the confectioners' sugar with 4 Tbsp [60 ml] of the milk and the anise liqueur. Continue to add the milk 1 Tbsp at a time to reach a runny glaze consistency. When the cookies are just barely still warm, brush the glaze over the top. Finish with a sprinkle of nonpareils.

The cooled cookies can be stored in an airtight container for up to 4 days.

ALMOND
MACAROON
COOKIES
PAGE 185

PIGNOLI
COOKIES
PAGE 188

BOW KNOT
COOKIES
PAGE 186

Pignoli COOKIES

MAKES / **ABOUT 18 COOKIES**

½ cup [100 g] granulated sugar

½ cup [60 g] confectioners' sugar, plus more for garnish

¼ cup [35 g] all-purpose flour, plus more as needed

One 8 oz [230 g] package almond paste, chilled

2 egg whites

1⅔ cups [200 g] pine nuts (about 7 oz)

Christmas Eve is the big holiday in my house, and to me, it's just not Christmas if the table isn't buckling under the weight of hundreds of cookies. Some people start baking weeks ahead and freeze everything, but I do everything the night before. My sisters Cookie and Fran, my daughter, my niece, and my sons' partners all gather the night before Christmas Eve, and we pull out all the stops. I'm usually up until two or three in the morning so everything is super fresh. The key with pignoli cookies is you want to serve them nice and warm—that's when they're the best.

Preheat the oven to 300°F [150°C]. Line two rimmed baking sheets with parchment paper.

In a food processor, combine the granulated sugar, confectioners' sugar, and flour. Pulse two times to combine. Crumble in small pieces of almond paste and pulse again to combine, about four times. With the processor running, add one egg white and let it incorporate. If the dough comes together, you can stop there. If it's still a little dry, add the remaining egg white. You can balance out with 1 or 2 Tbsp of flour to get a sticky but cohesive dough.

Pour the pine nuts into a small bowl. Use a 1 Tbsp measure to scoop the dough. Drop into the bowl of pine nuts and roll until it's lightly coated. Transfer to one of the prepared baking sheets. Continue scooping and rolling, spacing the cookies 2 in [5 cm] apart on the baking sheet. Bake for 20 to 24 minutes, until nicely golden brown. Transfer the cookies to a wire rack to cool. While one batch bakes, roll and shape the next batch onto the other baking sheet.

Just before serving, dust the slightly warm cookies with a little confectioners' sugar. The cookies can be stored in an airtight container for up to 4 days.

Struffoli

3 eggs

4 Tbsp [55 g] unsalted butter, melted

1 cup [200 g] sugar

Juice of ½ navel orange

1 tsp vanilla extract

3 cups [420 g] all-purpose flour, plus more for dusting

½ tsp baking powder

One 16 oz [455 g] container Crisco or 2 cups [480 ml] vegetable oil

1 cup [340 g] honey

Rainbow nonpareils, for garnish

This is an old family recipe that my grandmother used to make every Christmas. My sister Cookie took over from her and for years she was the struffoli master in our family. Eventually I took over and folded it into my Christmas Eve all-night cookie baking. True to tradition, I still make it only once a year, which means the competition gets fierce and a fight is going to break out as we finish every last piece. It's really that good! These struffoli are so light and airy but have a nice crunch on the outside. A little honey glaze is all they need so they're sweet, but not too sweet. I might be biased, but I've never had a better one!

In a large bowl, whisk together the eggs, butter, sugar, orange juice, and vanilla. Add the flour and baking powder and use a wooden spoon to stir into a soft dough.

Lightly dust a work surface with flour. Cut the dough into ten equal pieces and roll each one into ½ in [13 mm] wide ropes. Cut each rope into 1 in [2.5 cm] pieces and roll each piece into a ball. Set the balls on a rimmed baking sheet while rolling the rest.

In a medium saucepan, melt the Crisco or heat the vegetable oil. Use a fry thermometer to monitor the temperature. When the oil reaches 350°F [180°C], add a small batch of struffoli and fry, stirring occasionally, until they're puffy and golden brown, about 2 minutes. Transfer the fried struffoli to paper towels and continue frying the rest in batches.

In a small saucepan over low heat, warm the honey until it's runny. Add all the fried struffoli to a large bowl and spoon the honey over the top. Toss to coat, then stack the warm struffoli in a ring on a large serving platter. (The honey will help them stick together!) Drizzle any remaining honey over the top, then cover with nonpareils. Serve immediately while they're still warm.

STRUFFOLI
PAGE 189

DEEP-FRIED *Oreo* ICE CREAM SANDWICHES

SERVES / 8

1 cup [140 g] pancake mix

1 cup [240 ml] whole milk

1 egg

2 qt [1.9 L] plus 2 Tbsp vegetable oil

16 Oreo cookies

1 pint [480 ml] ice cream, any flavor

Confectioners' sugar, for dusting

Years ago, my sons were involved with running the food and beverages at a restaurant. This was a dessert on their menu that I absolutely loved. Same story as the Almond Macaroon Cookies (page 185): I can never catch a break around here and get a damn recipe, so I decided I would figure this one out myself, and I did! It reminds me so much of summers on the boardwalk down the shore. The crispy fried Oreos are a perfect sandwich for melting ice cream. It's junk, but the best kind. It just doesn't get better than this.

In a medium bowl, whisk the pancake mix, milk, egg, and 2 Tbsp of the vegetable oil into a smooth batter.

In a medium saucepan over medium heat, heat the remaining 2 qt [1.9 L] of vegetable oil. Use a fry thermometer to monitor the temperature. When the oil reaches 375°F [190°C], use a fork to dip a cookie into the batter to coat. Let some of the excess batter drip off, then lower the cookie into the oil. Continue coating and frying three more cookies. Fry until golden brown all over, flipping halfway through, 3 to 4 minutes. Remove the cookies to paper towels to drain. Continue battering and frying in batches of four while monitoring the oil temperature.

Arrange eight of the cookies on a serving platter. Place a scoop of ice cream on each, then top with a second cookie. Dust with a little confectioners' sugar before serving.

For an extra-special touch, I like to decorate the plate with a drizzle of raspberry sauce and chocolate syrup!

Chocolate
BARK

12 oz [340 g] chocolate,
chopped (your choice of
milk, semisweet, or dark)

1 Tbsp refined coconut oil

Toppings of choice (see
below)

◆◆◆◆◆◆◆◆◆◆◆◆◆◆◆◆◆◆◆◆◆◆◆◆◆

Chocolate bark, once you get
the hang of it, has endless
possibilities. I've listed some of
my favorite toppings, but really,
there are a million ways to do
it. It's a great treat around the
holidays and I'm constantly
making baggies to hand out. This
is also the kind of easy recipe
you can share with the kids. It's
one of the things I taught my
granddaughter to show her that
cooking is easy and fun.

◆◆◆◆◆◆◆◆◆◆◆◆◆◆◆◆◆◆◆◆◆◆◆◆◆

Line a rimmed baking sheet with parchment paper. Lightly coat
the parchment with nonstick spray.

Set a small saucepan with 1 in [2.5 cm] of water over medium
heat. When the water is simmering, set a medium bowl over
the saucepan, making sure it doesn't touch the water. Add the
chopped chocolate and coconut oil. Let the heat slowly melt
the chocolate, stirring occasionally to incorporate the coconut
oil. When the mixture is completely smooth, about 4 minutes,
remove from the heat. Stir in your toppings of choice, leaving
about half for garnish.

Scrape the mixture onto the prepared baking sheet and smooth
into an even layer. Sprinkle the remaining toppings over the
chocolate. Refrigerate for at least 2 hours, until set, or overnight.
Break into large pieces before serving.

Topping
IDEAS

ADD ANY
COMBINATION OF:

Toasted and chopped
macadamia nuts, hazelnuts,
walnuts, pecans, or almonds

Toasted sesame seeds or
pepitas

Toasted shredded coconut

Dried cherries, cranberries,
chopped dried apricots,
or chopped dried figs

Crushed peppermint candies

Chopped candied citrus or
crystalized ginger

Crushed pretzels, graham
crackers, or potato chips

About 1½ cups [360 g] total
is the perfect amount.

Peanut BRITTLE

SERVES / 8

1 cup [200 g] sugar

½ cup [160 g] light corn syrup

⅛ tsp kosher salt

1 cup [140 g] dry-roasted peanuts

2 Tbsp unsalted butter

2 tsp vanilla extract

1 tsp baking soda

I love peanut brittle. It's the perfect sweet-savory balance. The problem is it's so expensive to buy in stores, which is, frankly, dumb. Look at that ingredient list; there's nothing special there! So I started making my own instead. There's nothing better than being able to whip up your favorite treat on demand.

Coat a rimmed baking sheet with nonstick spray.

In a medium saucepan over medium heat, combine the sugar and corn syrup without stirring. Let the mixture come to a boil, again without stirring. Boil until it reaches 280°F [138°C] on a candy thermometer, about 5 minutes.

Stir in the salt and peanuts and cook until it reaches 310°F [154°C], about 2 minutes longer. The mixture should be nicely golden brown. Remove from the heat and whisk in the butter, vanilla, and baking soda. Pour the mixture onto the prepared baking sheet. Let sit until hardened, about 5 minutes. Break into large pieces. The brittle can be stored in an airtight container for up to 5 days.

Poached APPLES

WITH
BRANDY SAUCE

SERVES / 4

2 cups [480 ml] unsweetened
    apple juice

1/2 cup [120 ml] brandy

2 cinnamon sticks

Pinch of ground nutmeg

Pinch of ground cloves

4 Red Delicious apples,
    peeled, halved, and cored

Toasted chopped hazelnuts,
    for garnish

Brace yourself, things are about to get weird. My dad's dad loved to eat poached apples with pig's feet. When I was young, my stomach would flip when I was poaching apples because I knew that meant I would have to open the jar and fish a foot out. Luckily, that trauma passed and mostly I remembered the smell of the apples as they were poaching, which is truly the best fall smell that fills the entire house. So as an adult, I'm reclaiming the poached apples and doing it my way (no feet whatsoever). I think brandy is underused in desserts; its boozy sweetness is especially good here as a warm sauce over the soft apples.

Set a large saucepan on a piece of parchment paper. Trace a circle the size of the pan, then cut it out. Fold the circle in half and cut a small crescent from the center so there's a hole in the center of the parchment circle.

In the same saucepan, combine the apple juice, brandy, cinnamon sticks, nutmeg, and cloves. Set over medium heat and bring the liquid to a simmer. Add the apple halves and set the parchment round over the top, pressing onto the surface of the liquid. (This will help keep the apples submerged and evenly poached.)

Turn the heat to low and gently simmer for 15 minutes. Peel away the parchment and flip the apples. Return the parchment and continue simmering for 10 to 15 minutes, until a paring knife easily slides in and out of an apple.

Discard the parchment and cinnamon sticks. Use a spider strainer or slotted spoon to remove the apples to serving bowls. Increase the heat to high and boil the liquid until it reduces by half, about 4 minutes. Spoon the hot liquid over the apples and garnish with hazelnuts just before serving.

**This is also excellent
with a scoop of ice
cream or a big dollop of
whipped cream!**

SPIKED *Fruit Salad*

WITH

MASCARPONE DIP

SERVES / 10

FRUIT SALAD

3/4 cup [180 ml] anisette liqueur

1/2 cup [120 ml] orange juice

1 pineapple, peeled, cored, and sliced

3 medium oranges, peeled and separated into wedges

2 medium Bosc pears, cored and sliced

2 medium Granny Smith apples, cored and sliced

MASCARPONE DIP

One 8 oz [230 g] package mascarpone, at room temperature

1/4 cup [60 ml] heavy cream

1/2 cup [60 g] confectioners' sugar

Pinch of ground cinnamon

This humble fruit salad gets a serious upgrade, thanks to a little splash of alcohol and decadent dip. I like anisette liqueur, a sweet liqueur popular in the Mediterranean, such as pastis in France, ouzo in Greece, and sambuca in Italy. The liqueur is already sweet, so the savory herbal anise flavor plays off everything perfectly. Right before serving, I whip up an easy mascarpone dip to serve with the cold fruit. There's truly nothing better on a hot day!

TO MAKE THE FRUIT SALAD: In a large bowl, whisk together the liqueur and orange juice. Add the fruit and toss to coat. Cover with plastic wrap and refrigerate for at least 2 hours before serving or up to 6 hours.

JUST BEFORE SERVING, MAKE THE MASCARPONE DIP: In a small bowl, whisk together the mascarpone and heavy cream until combined and soft. Add the confectioners' sugar and whisk until combined. This can also be made ahead and chilled, but let it sit at room temperature for 30 minutes before serving. Sprinkle the cinnamon over the dip just before serving.

Late Night Snacks

◆◆◆◆◆◆◆◆◆◆◆

When those bottles of wine somehow finished themselves or the stomach just needs a couple more bites before bed, these late night snacks come to the rescue with savory and sweet (and a few boozy) nibbles, ready in a flash, to send you off to dreamland.

Spaghetti AGLIO E OLIO

SERVES / 4

1 lb [455 g] spaghetti or angel hair pasta

½ cup [120 ml] extra-virgin olive oil

4 garlic cloves, smashed

¼ cup [10 g] finely chopped fresh parsley

3 Tbsp chicken stock

½ cup [30 g] grated pecorino or ½ cup [15 g] Parmesan cheese, plus more for serving

Kosher salt

Red pepper flakes

This is hands-down my boys' favorite dish and, lucky for me, this is just about the easiest thing I could make. The list of ingredients is basically a list of things I have in stock at all times, and it comes together so fast. The preparation is basically just boiling pasta, browning garlic, then grabbing your biggest bowl and tossing it all together. I like to add a splash of chicken stock—my culinary secret weapon—for extra richness, plus a pile of salty cheese to make everything creamy and well seasoned. When it's this simple, I'm happy to make it by popular demand any night of the week!

Bring a large pot of salted water to a boil over high heat. Cook the pasta to al dente, according to the package directions. Drain well and transfer to a large bowl.

In a large skillet over medium heat, heat the olive oil. When the oil shimmers, add the garlic. Sauté until the garlic is just starting to brown, about 4 minutes. Immediately pour the oil and garlic over the pasta. Add the parsley, chicken stock, and cheese and toss to combine. Taste for seasoning, adding salt as needed. Serve immediately with more grated cheese and a sprinkle of red pepper flakes.

NOTE

Don't microwave leftover pasta! Add it to a skillet with a splash of water, set over medium heat, and toss until warmed through.

Homemade TRUFFLE POPCORN

(SERVES / 4)

4 Tbsp [55 g] unsalted butter, melted and cooled

2 Tbsp truffle oil

1/4 cup [8 g] grated Parmesan cheese

1/4 cup [10 g] finely chopped fresh parsley

1/2 cup [100 g] popcorn kernels

Truffle salt or kosher salt

◆◆◆◆◆◆◆◆◆◆◆◆◆◆◆◆◆◆◆◆◆◆◆◆

My family loves a bag of microwave popcorn more than almost any snack. Over the years, we've spent a lot of time experimenting with our favorite add-ins, but I have to say nothing beats the smell of this truffle popcorn. It's an easy combo of butter and truffle oil, plus I like to mix in some cheese, parsley, and a final sprinkle of truffle salt. But use whatever you have; there are no wrong answers here. I'm including my hack for homemade microwave popcorn that's just as easy to make as the store-bought bag. Trust me, it'll change the way you make popcorn forever!

◆◆◆◆◆◆◆◆◆◆◆◆◆◆◆◆◆◆◆◆◆◆◆◆

In a small bowl, whisk together the butter, truffle oil, Parmesan, and parsley.

Add the popcorn kernels to a brown paper lunch bag. Fold the top of the bag twice to seal tightly. Place the bag in the microwave and microwave on high for 2 to 3 minutes, until there are 2-second pauses between pops. Remove the bag and carefully open the top. Pour in the butter mixture, fold the bag, and shake to incorporate. Pour the popcorn into a bowl and season with salt before serving.

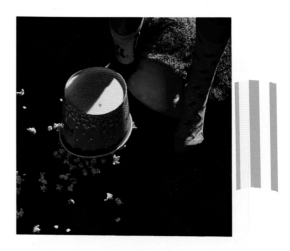

MOZZARELLA IN *Carrozza*

MAKES / 2 SANDWICHES

4 pieces thinly sliced prosciutto, chopped

½ cup [40 g] shredded low-moisture mozzarella

¼ cup [15 g] grated pecorino

6 sun-dried tomatoes, drained and chopped

1 egg

½ cup [70 g] seasoned bread crumbs

4 slices white sandwich bread, crusts trimmed

½ cup [120 ml] extra-virgin olive oil

This is like grilled cheese on steroids. I like mine with a piece of prosciutto and chopped sun-dried tomatoes, but swap in anything you're craving. All that matters is you load it up with plenty of melty mozzarella, coat it in bread crumbs, and fry it until it's golden and crispy on the outside and totally gooey on the inside. When it's late and you need a greasy snack, it doesn't get better than this!

In a medium bowl, combine the prosciutto, mozzarella, pecorino, and sun-dried tomatoes. In a medium shallow bowl, whisk the egg. In a separate shallow bowl, spread the bread crumbs in an even layer.

Arrange the bread on a cutting board. Divide the cheese mixture between two of the slices. Press the other two slices on top, then press firmly around the edges to seal the bread. Dip one sandwich into the egg, coating both sides and letting the excess drip off. Drop into the bread crumbs and sprinkle the bread crumbs to cover. Press and flip to make sure the sandwich is fully covered, then transfer back to the cutting board. Repeat with the second sandwich.

In a large skillet over low heat, heat the olive oil. Test the oil by dipping an edge of a coated sandwich into the oil. If the oil bubbles nicely, it's ready to fry. Place both of the sandwiches in the skillet. Fry for about 3 minutes per side, until golden brown all over. Transfer back to the cutting board and slice diagonally before serving.

English Muffin PIZZA

SERVES 1

1 English muffin, split and toasted

4 Tbsp [60 ml] pizza sauce or marinara sauce

½ cup [40 g] shredded mozzarella cheese, or 2 slices American cheese

This English muffin pizza was a staple in my house growing up, it was a staple when my kids were growing up, and now my granddaughter asks for it when she comes over too. When I was little, my mom would send us out in the snow to play. When our energy had finally burned off and we trudged back in, she would take our boots off, wrap us in a towel, and send us to the kitchen where Star Soup (page 74) and English muffin pizzas were waiting. All these years later, when I make this simple little pizza for my own family, my heart still smiles.

Preheat the oven to 400°F [200°C].

Arrange the toasted muffin halves on a rimmed baking sheet. Spread 2 Tbsp [30 ml] of the sauce on each half, then pile ¼ cup [20 g] of the cheese over each. Bake for 8 to 10 minutes until the cheese is melted and gooey. As an optional step, set the broiler to high. Slide the sheet under the broiler and broil for 1 to 2 minutes until the cheese is golden brown. Serve immediately.

The Special

SERVES / 1

When my son Albie was little, I would make him a bologna and cheese sandwich for school every day. It was a routine we both looked forward to. And when he got home in the afternoon, he always asked for a triple-decker peanut butter sandwich for an after-school snack. One morning I went to make his sandwich and realized I didn't have bologna in the fridge, so I panicked and made him a peanut butter sandwich instead. I was sick to my stomach all day because he didn't have his usual sandwich. (He was and still is a creature of habit.) But when he got home that day, he said, "Mom! I can't believe you made me The Special!" All my mom-worrying was for nothing; it was the best day of his life. (But the next day I went back to bologna just to be safe.)

3 slices white sandwich bread
Peanut butter

Lay the slices of bread on a cutting board. Spread peanut butter evenly on each slice. Stack the slices on top of each other, with the peanut butter facing up for the bottom and center layer and facing down for the top layer. Cut in half and serve.

NUTELLA *Pizza*

SERVES / **4 TO 8**

This is a very untraditional Italian classic. But when it's this delicious, who cares? It's an easy dessert and always a hit with the kids (or kids at heart), with its mix of Nutella, fresh fruit, and simple raspberry glaze. For me, there's no better combo than fruit and chocolate. Whenever I'm doing a pizza night, I always set some dough aside to make this, late into the night, as a grand finale.

1 lb [455 g] store-bought pizza dough

2 Tbsp unsalted butter, melted

3/4 cup [280 g] Nutella

Fresh fruit of choice (I generally use bananas, strawberries, raspberries, and blueberries), for topping

Fresh mint leaves, for garnish (optional)

Confectioners' sugar, for garnish

1 recipe Raspberry Glaze (recipe follows)

Preheat the oven to 450°F [230°C]. Line a rimmed baking sheet with aluminum foil and lightly grease.

Lightly dust a work surface with flour and roll out the pizza dough into a rough rectangle, about 10 by 14 in [25 by 35.5 cm]. It doesn't have to be perfect. Transfer to the prepared baking sheet and dimple the dough all over with your fingers. Brush with the butter and bake for about 10 minutes, until the crust is golden brown.

Remove from the oven and spread the Nutella over the pizza. Slice the fruit as needed and spread evenly over the pie. Arrange some fresh mint (if using) and very lightly dust with confectioners' sugar. Spoon about 1/4 cup [60 ml] of the raspberry glaze over the pizza and serve the rest of the glaze on the side for dipping.

RASPBERRY GLAZE

MAKES 1½ CUPS [360 ML]

2 cups [240 g] raspberries, fresh or frozen

6 Tbsp [65 g] sugar

2 Tbsp fresh lemon juice

In a blender, combine the raspberries, sugar, and lemon juice. Blend until smooth, about 1 minute. Set a fine-mesh strainer over a medium bowl. Pour the glaze through and use a rubber spatula to stir. Discard the seeds.

CHOCOLATE CHIP Cookies

MAKES / **ABOUT 20 COOKIES**

My sister Fran is the queen of the chocolate chip cookie. I got the cooking genes and she got the baking genes, so I defer to her expertise when it comes to anything sweet. This is Fran's recipe and it's perfect in every way. The cookies are crispy on the edges, chewy in the center, perfectly chocolaty, and a little crunchy with the pecan and coconut. I've been making them for decades and they never fail.

1 cup [226 g] unsalted butter, at room temperature

3/4 cup [150 g] granulated sugar

3/4 cup [150 g] packed light brown sugar

2 eggs

1½ tsp vanilla extract

2¾ cups [385 g] all-purpose flour

1 tsp kosher salt

1 tsp baking soda

2 cups [360 g] semisweet chocolate chips

1 cup [120 g] chopped pecans (optional)

½ cup [40 g] unsweetened shredded coconut (optional)

Preheat the oven to 350°F [180°C]. Line two rimmed baking sheets with parchment paper.

In a large bowl, use a handheld mixer at medium speed to cream together the butter, granulated sugar, and brown sugar. Add the eggs one at a time, beating until each one is incorporated. Beat in the vanilla. Sift in the flour, salt, and baking soda. Use a rubber spatula to fold until just a few streaks remain. Fold in the chocolate chips, pecans (if using), and coconut (if using).

Use a 3 Tbsp cookie scoop to form about half of the dough into balls (about the size of a golf ball). Set on the prepared baking sheet and press down lightly to flatten, leaving about 1 in [2.5 cm] between each cookie. Bake for about 15 minutes, until golden brown. Cool on the baking sheet for about 5 minutes, then transfer the cookies to a wire rack to cool. While the first batch is baking, scoop the remaining dough onto the second baking sheet and transfer to the oven when the first batch comes out. Serve the cookies while still warm.

 **N·O·T·E** The cookies can be frozen before baking. After scooping and pressing, transfer the entire baking sheet to the freezer until the dough is completely solid. Transfer the individual cookies to a zip-top bag and freeze for up to 2 months. Just add 2 to 5 minutes to the bake time and you'll have cookies on demand as a late night snack. (Even if it's just a single freshly baked cookie!)

ADULT
ROOT BEER
FLOAT
PAGE 217

Hot Toddy

This is my favorite end to a cold night. It always sends me to bed feeling warm and sleepy. My daughter, Lauren, introduced these to the family because if there's alcohol around, she'll find a way to make something delicious with it. She has played with a million versions over the years, but for me, the classic is still the best.

4 whole cloves

2 lemon wedges

Boiling water

1/2 tsp honey

2 oz [60 ml] bourbon or Irish whiskey

Stick the cloves into one of the lemon wedges. Fill a mug with boiling water and squeeze the juice of the other lemon wedge into the mug. Stir in the honey and bourbon. Float the clove wedge on the top before serving.

Adult ROOT BEER Float

This was a Christopher invention after a late night of drinking. I have to say, it's how a root beer float should always be served. (To adults, obviously.) It's all the classic flavors, but with just a little hit of booze, and it's delicious. I like to use Not Your Father's brand of root beer, but grab whatever you can find!

1 pint [480 ml] vanilla ice cream

Two 12 oz [360 ml] bottles spiked root beer, very cold

Whipped cream, for serving

Freeze two tall float glasses for 30 minutes, until frosty. Place a few big scoops of ice cream in each glass. Tilt the glasses at an angle and slowly pour the cold root beer over the ice cream. Top with a swirl of whipped cream and serve with a spoon and a straw.

Acknowledgments

◆◆◆◆◆◆◆◆◆◆◆◆◆◆◆◆◆◆◆◆◆◆◆◆◆◆◆◆◆◆◆◆◆◆

I would be remiss if I didn't acknowledge the wonderful
team of people who turned my dream into reality.

◆◆◆◆◆◆◆◆◆◆◆◆◆◆◆◆◆◆◆◆◆◆◆◆◆◆◆◆◆◆◆◆◆◆

ELLEN SCORDATO and **THE STONESONG TEAM,** thank you for having faith in me and working so hard to find the perfect match for my book. You were the start of a dream, and I thank you.

To **THE CHRONICLE TEAM:** Dena Rayess and Cristina Garces, my editors, you took a chance on me, and I'll be forever grateful. Thank you for making my dream come true. I promise to make you proud!

LIZZIE VAUGHAN, thank you for art directing a book that makes me smile every time I open it. You captured my personality perfectly.

LAURA PALESE, thank you for your incredible design work. It's fun, it's happy, it's food, it's family, it's me. Thank you, thank you, thank you.

ELORA SULLIVAN, ERICA GELBARD, and **LAUREN HOFFMAN,** for your tireless efforts to get me and my book out there for all to see! Thank you!

LAUREN VOLO, I always say my food isn't pretty, but it's good. Somehow your photos make my food look so pretty! Miracles can happen!

MIRA IRVINE, I don't know how you do it, cooking each dish under a deadline and making it look awesome for the camera. You are a treasure!

MEGAN LITT and **SOLI ZARDOSHT,** you are both adorable and super hard workers. I see you and appreciate you both. Thank you!

MAEVE SHERIDAN, you and all your pretty things along with your eye for creativity made this process so fun, and the photos pop. Thank you!

ASHLEE HOLMES, thank you for making your old Aunt Caroline look pretty! Love you!

CASEY ELSASS, I have no words. I gave you a binder full of recipes and you brought them to life. This book WOULD. NOT. BE. HERE. without you. A thousand thank you's would never be enough. But I will start with just one THANK YOU. xo

For all the memories made around the table, and in the kitchen. For friends and family who are no longer with us, and those who are here and continue to fill my life with joy. Every single recipe in this book reflects each of you and our time spent together. Each page is filled with love and gratitude. It is my hope that generations that follow continue with the tradition of food, love, and togetherness. I love you all, thank you.

Index